The Young and the Restless Cast Party: An Unauthorized Guide to the History, Characters, and Cast of One of the Most Popular Soap Operas

Calista King

The role of the book within our culture is changing. The change is brought on by new ways to acquire & use content, the rapid dissemination of information and real-time peer collaboration on a global scale. Despite these changes one thing is clear--"the book" in it's traditional form continues to play an important role in learning and communication. The book you are holding in your hands utilizes the unique characteristics of the Internet -- relying on web infrastructure and collaborative tools to share and use resources in keeping with the characteristics of the medium (user-created, defying control, etc.)--while maintaining all the convenience and utility of a real book.

Contents

Articles

References

All the Facts: The Young and the Restless

The Young and the Restless

The Young and the Restless	
Genre	Soap opera
Creator(s)	William J. Bell Lee Philip Bell
Senior cast member(s)	Jeanne Cooper Doug Davidson Melody Thomas Scott Eric Braeden Eileen Davidson Kate Linder Tracey E. Bregman Jess Walton Peter Bergman Kristoff St. John
Country of origin	United States
Language(s)	English
No. of episodes	9,465 (as of September 17, 2010)
Production	
Executive producer(s)	Maria Arena Bell (co-executive producer) Paul Rauch (co-executive producer)
Head writer(s)	Maria Arena Bell, Hogan Sheffer and Scott Hamner
Distributor	Bell Dramatic Serial Company and Corday Productions, Inc. in association with Sony Pictures Television (Columbia TriStar Television 2001 until 2002, Columbia Pictures Television 1974 to 2001, and Screen Gems until name change in 1974)

Running time	30 minutes (1973–1980)
	60 minutes (1980–present)
Broadcast	
Original channel	CBS
Original run	March 26, 1973 – present
External links	
Official website [1]	

The Young and the Restless is an American television soap opera created by William J. Bell and Lee Phillip Bell for CBS. The show is set in a fictional Wisconsin town called Genoa City, which is unlike and unrelated to the real life village of the same name, Genoa City, Wisconsin. First broadcast on March 26, 1973, *The Young and the Restless* was originally broadcast as half-hour episodes, five times a week. It expanded to one hour episodes on February 4, 1980. In 2006 the show began airing on weeknights SOAPnet. The series is also syndicated internationally.

The Young and the Restless originally focuses on two core families, the wealthy Brooks family and the poor Foster family. After a series of recasts and departures, in the early 1980s all the original characters except Jill Foster Abbott were written out. Bell replaced them with the new core families, the Abbotts and the Williams'. Over the years, other families such as the Newmans and the Winters were introduced. Despite these changes, one storyline that has endured through almost the show's entire run is the feud between Jill Foster Abbott and Katherine Chancellor, the longest rivalries on any American soap opera.

Since its debut, *The Young and the Restless* has won seven Daytime Emmy Awards for Outstanding Drama Series. It is also currently the highest-rated daytime drama on American television. As of 2008, it has appeared at the top of the weekly Nielsen ratings in that category for more than 1,000 weeks since 1988.

Production

To compete with the youthful ABC soap operas, *All My Children*, *One Life to Live*, and *General Hospital*, CBS executives wanted a new daytime serial that was youth oriented. William J. Bell and Lee Phillip Bell created *The Young and the Restless* in 1972 for the network under the working title, *The Innocent Years!* "We were confronted with the very disturbing reality that young America had lost much of its innocence," Bell said. "Innocence as we had known and lived it all our lives had, in so many respects, ceased to exist." They changed the title of the series to *The Young and the Restless* because they felt it "reflected the youth and mood of the early seventies." The Bells named the fictional setting for the show after the real Genoa City, Wisconsin, which was located on their way from their then-home in Chicago to their annual summer vacation spot in Lake Geneva.

The Young and the Restless began airing on March 26, 1973, replacing the canceled soap opera, *Where the Heart Is*. Bell worked as head writer from the debut of the series until his retirement in 1998. He wrote from his home in Chicago while production took place in Los Angeles, California. John Conboy acted as the show's first executive producer, staying in the position until 1982. Bell and H. Wesley Kenney became co-executive producers that year until Edward Scott took over in 1989. Bell then became senior executive producer. Other executive producers included David Shaughnessy, John F. Smith, Lynn Marie Latham, Josh Griffith, Maria Arena Bell, and Paul Rauch.

In the mid-1980s, Bell and his family moved to Los Angeles to create a new soap opera. During this time, his three children, William Jr., Bradley, and Lauralee Bell, each became involved in soap operas. Lauralee Bell worked as an actress on *The Young and the Restless*. Bradley Bell co-created *The Bold and the Beautiful* with his father. William Bell Jr. became involved in the family's production companies as president of Bell Dramatic Serial Co. and Bell-Phillip Television Productions Inc. "It's worked out very well for us because we really all worked in very different aspects of the show," William Bell Jr. said. "With my father and I, it was a great kind of partnership and pairing in the sense that he had a total control of the creative side of the show and I didn't have even the inclination to interject in what he was doing."

After William J. Bell's 1998 retirement, a number of different head writers took over the position, including Kay Alden, Trent Jones, John F. Smith, Lynn Marie Latham, Scott Hamner, Josh Griffith, Maria Arena Bell, and Hogan Sheffer.

Filming and broadcasting

Taped at CBS Television City in Los Angeles since its debut on March 26, 1973, the show was packaged by the distribution company Columbia Pictures Television. *The Young and the Restless* originally aired as a half-hour series on CBS and was the first soap opera to focus on the visual aspects of production, creating "a look that broke with the visual conventions of the genre." Similar to radio shows, soap operas at the time primarily focused on dialogue, characters, and story, with details like sets as secondary concerns. *The Young and the Restless* stood out by using unique lighting techniques and camera angles, similar to Hollywood-style productions. The style of filming included using out of the ordinary camera angles and a large amount of facial close-ups with bright lighting on the actors' faces. Conboy said he used lighting to create "artistic effects". Those effects made the series look dark, shadowy, and moody. *The Young and the Restless'* look influenced the filming styles of other soap operas. When H. Wesley Kenney replaced Conboy as executive producer, he balanced the lighting of the scenes.

Due to the success of the series, CBS and their affiliates pressured Bell to lengthen the series from 30 minutes to a full hour. Bell attributed this change to the show's fall from number one in the Nielsen ratings, since the lengthening of the show led to the departure of a number of cast members. "The issue of performing in a one-hour show had not been part of their contracts," Bell said. This forced the show to recast multiple main characters and eventually phase out the original core families in favor of new ones.

On June 27, 2001, *The Young and the Restless* became the first daytime soap opera to be broadcast in high-definition. On April 24, 2006, SoapNet began airing same-day episodes of the series.

Casting and story development

See also: List of The Young and the Restless cast members and List of The Young and the Restless characters

Co-creators William J. Bell and Lee Phillip Bell centered *The Young and the Restless* around two core families, the wealthy Brooks' and the poor Fosters. Bell borrowed this technique of soap opera building from his mentor, Irna Phillips.

While casting for the series, Bell and executive producer John Conboy auditioned 540 actors for the 13 main characters. They assembled the youngest group of actors ever cast on a soap opera at the time, hiring mostly unknown actors who they considered "glamorous model types". Chemistry between actors also factored into the criteria for casting. The stories focused on the younger characters, with an emphasis in fantasy. The fantasy element was reflected in the love story between Jill Foster and the millionaire Phillip Chancellor II; the Leslie Brooks, Brad Elliot, and Laurie Brooks love triangle; and Snapper Foster's romance with Chris Brooks.

Sexuality also played a major role in the stories. Formerly, soap operas did not delve into the sexual side of their romances. Bell changed that, first during his time as head writer of *Days of our Lives* and again on *The Young and the Restless*. William Gray Espy's Snapper Foster is considered the "first to discover sex on a soap opera." During the story, the character is engaged to Chris Brooks (Trish Stewart) and having a sexual relationship with Sally McGuire (Lee Crawford). Other plots reflected sexual themes as well. For the first time in the genre, the dialogue and the story situations included explicit sexual themes such as premarital intercourse, impotence, incest, and rape. The series also explored social issues. Jennifer Brooks underwent the first mastectomy on a soap opera. Other social issue storylines included bulimia, alcoholism, and cancer. Lesbianism was also touched on with Katherine Chancellor, who flirts with Jill while drunk in 1974 and has a brief relationship with Joann Curtis (Kay Heberle) in 1977.

When the series lengthened from a half hour to an hour in 1980, multiple cast members who portrayed characters from the original core families departed because their contracts only bound them to performing in a half hour show. A number of the characters were recast until one of the few remaining original actors, Jamie Lyn Bauer, who portrayed Lauralee Brooks, decided to leave. When she announced her intention not to renew her contract, Bell decided to replace the original core families. "As I studied the remaining cast, I realized I had two characters- Paul Williams, played by Doug Davidson, and Jack Abbott, played by Terry Lester- both of whom had a relatively insignificant presence on the show," Bell said. "They didn't have families. Hell, they didn't even have bedrooms. But these became the two characters I would build our two families around."

The characters from the Abbott and Williams families were integrated into the series while the Brooks and Foster families, with the exception of Jill, were phased out. The continuity of the feud between Jill and Katherine, which began in the early years of the show, smoothed the transition. The relationship between the two characters remained a central theme throughout the series and became the longest lasting rivalry in daytime history.

Another character introduced in the 1980s was Eric Braeden's Victor Newman. Originally, the character was "a despicable, contemptible, unfaithful wife abuser" who was intended to be killed off. Braeden's tenure on the show was meant to last between eight and twelve weeks. "When I saw Eric Braeden's first performance- the voice, the power, the inner strength- I knew immediately that I didn't want to lose this man," Bell said. "He was exactly what the show needed. Not the hateful man we saw on-screen, but the man he could and would become." Bell rewrote the story to save the character and put Braeden on contract. Victor's romance with Nikki Reed became a prominent plot in the series.

In the 1990s, core black characters were introduced with the Barber and Winters families. Victoria Rowell (Drucilla Barber) and Tonya Lee Williams (Dr. Olivia Barber) were cast as the nieces of the Abbott's maid, Mamie Johnson, in 1990. The brothers Neil (Kristoff St. John) and Malcolm Winters (Shemar Moore) were introduced as love interests for Olivia and Drucilla. *The Young and the Restless* became popular among black viewers, which Williams and St. John attributed to the writing for the black characters. "I play a CEO at a major corporation, that's something we don't see that often," St. John said. "And the show doesn't use the old African-American stereotypes that we have been seeing on TV, like the hustler, the pimp, the drug dealer. We have come a long way." Though the characters held prominent positions in the fictional work place of Genoa City, they had little interaction with other characters outside of their jobs.

Awards

The serial has won 100 Daytime Emmys, along with 334 nominations. The following list summarizes awards won by *The Young and the Restless*:

Daytime Emmy Awards

Category	Recipient	Role	Year(s)
Outstanding Drama Series			1975, 1983, 1985, 1986, 1993, 2004, 2007
Outstanding Individual Director in a Daytime Drama Series	Richard Dunlap		1975, 1978
Outstanding Drama Series Directing Team			1986, 1987, 1988, 1989, 1996, 1997, 1998, 1999, 2000, 2001, 2002
Outstanding Drama Series Writing Team			1992, 1997, 2006,
Lead Actor	Peter Bergman Eric Braeden Christian LeBlanc	Jack Abbott Victor Newman Michael Baldwin	1991, 1992, 2002 1998 2005, 2007 2009
Lead Actress	Jess Walton Michelle Stafford Jeanne Cooper	Jill Foster Abbott Phyllis Summers Katherine Chancellor	1997 2004 2008
Supporting Actor	Shemar Moore Greg Rikaart Kristoff St. John Billy Miller	Malcolm Winters Kevin Fisher Neil Winters Billy Abbott	2000 2005 2008 2010
Supporting Actress	Beth Maitland Jess Walton Michelle Stafford Sharon Case	Traci Abbott Connolly Jill Foster Abbott Phyllis Summers Sharon Newman	1985 1991 1997 1999
Younger Actress	Tracey E. Bregman Tricia Cast Heather Tom Camryn Grimes	Lauren Fenmore Nina Webster Victoria Newman Cassie Newman	1985 1992 1993, 1999 2000
Younger Actor	Kristoff St. John David Tom David Lago Bryton James	Neil Winters Billy Abbott Raul Guittierez Devon Hamilton	1992 2000 2005 2007

TV Soap Golden Boomerang Awards

- 2006 "Hall of Fame Inductee" Eric Braeden (Victor Newman)

Writers Guild of America Awards

- 2003 "Best Daytime Serial" Written by Kay Alden, Trent Jones, John F. Smith, Jerry Birn, Jim Houghton, Natalie Minardi, Janice Ferri, Eric Freiwald, Joshua McCaffrey, Michael Minnis, Rex M. Best
- 2006 "Best Daytime Serial" Written by Kay Alden, John F. Smith, Janice Ferri, Jim Houghton, Natalie Minardi Slater, Sally Sussman Morina, Sara Bibel, Eric Freiwald, Linda Schreiber, Joshua S. McCaffrey, Marc Hertz, Sandra Weintraub
- 2008 "Best Daytime Serial" Written by Lynn Marie Latham, Scott Hamner, Bernard Lechowick, Cherie Bennett, Jeff Gottesfeld, Jim Stanley, Natalie Minardi Slater, Lynsey Dufour, Marina Alburger, Sara Bibel, Sandra Weintraub

Broadcasts outside the United States

In Australia, *The Young and the Restless* airs on Foxtel's W. Channel at 12 pm, and on the timeshift channel, W2, at 2 pm. Repeats of each day's episode air the following morning at 7:10 am and an omnibus edition airs at 8:10 am on Saturdays. It previously aired on Channel Nine from April 1, 1974 to February 23, 2007, before joining the W. line-up on April 2, 2007. Episodes are 9 months behind those airing in the US at present.

Main article: Screening of daytime soap operas in Australia

In Belgium, the show airs on RTBF-La Une as "Les Feux de l'Amour" at 12:00 (dubbed in French) and is 3 years behind the U.S.

- In Belize, Channel 5 Great Belize Television airs it on schedule with the US at 1:00 pm Central Time. Rival Channel 7 Tropical Vision Limited airs on schedule as well at 2:00 pm, Central Time.

In Brazil, the show aired on Sony Entertainment Television for a brief time during the 1990s.

In Mexico, Cablevision on American Network channel 475

In Canada, Global TV airs new episodes a day ahead of CBS in the United States. Most Global stations use *The Young and the Restless* as a late-afternoon lead-in for their local newscasts[citation needed], but times vary by market. It also airs on NTV in Newfoundland and Labrador which airs new episodes one day ahead, and on E! (Canada) in Kelowna, British Columbia, which is not one day ahead.

- In the French-speaking province of Quebec, a dubbed version airs on TVA, with the title *Les Feux de l'amour* (Fires of Love), about eight years after initial airing.

- In Cyprus the show started from the 1986 season in June 1992 from private channel ANT1 Cyprus and continued until 2002 when ANT1 decided to drop all its foreign soap operas after the end of *Santa Barbara*.

In Finland the show airs on MTV3 under the title *Tunteita ja tuoksuja* ("Senses and scents").

In France, the show screens on TF1 as "Les Feux de l'Amour" (*Fires of Love*) at 13:55, since August 16, 1989. The show started from episode #3263 (aired on CBS on January 10, 1986), so the first 13 years were never viewed. The episodes are currently 3.5 years behind the US.

In Germany, the show aired on ZDF from March to December 2008. The network canceled the show because of bad ratings. The episodes were two years behind the US and the show is known as *Schatten der Leidenschaft* (*Shadows of the Passion*).

In Greece, the show airs on ET1 (Public TV Channel) at 17:00. Episodes are six years behind the US. It's known as *Ατίθασα νιάτα* (Atithasa niata) (literally *Untameable Youth*).

In India, the show began airing in February, 2007 on Zee Cafe at 20:00. The channel started with episodes from 2004.

In Italy, the show aired till October 2009 on Rete 4, using the Italian title Febbre d'amore *(Love Fever)*. Episodes were three years behind the US. *The Young and the Restless'* first Italian broadcast was in 1983.

In Jamaica, the show airs on CVMTV at 7pm.

In the Republic of Macedonia, episodes from 1998 and 1999 were shown on Sitel TV a couple of years ago. Currently, reruns are shown.

In New Zealand, *The Young and the Restless* used to air on TV ONE. Episodes were four years behind the US.

In Romania, the show airs on ProTV at 16:00 as "Tânăr şi neliniştit" and it is around 5 years behind the show in the U.S.

In Norway, *The Young and the Restless* aired on FEM (TV channel) from 2007−2008 .

In Poland, *The Young and the Restless* aired from September 1997 to August 2000 on Polsat, with 780 episodes broadcast. On September 1, 2008 the network began airing the show again, starting with episode 7090 from March 2001. The Polish title is *Żar młodości*, which translates into *Fervor of Youth*.

In Philippines, aired from 1987 to 1989 on ABS-CBN.

In Serbia, B92 aired the show briefly in 2007, as "Mladi i nestašni". It also aired on TV Palma for a period of time in the 1990s, titled "Mladi i nemirni".

In Slovenia, the show airs on Kanal A as *Mladi in nemirni*. Episodes currently air from the first half of 2007.

In South Africa, the show airs on e.tv at 17:10. *The Young and the Restless* was moved from the 17:30 timeslot to the 17:10 timeslot, after *Passions* was canceled in South Africa on September 12,

2008. The show was originally aired in South Africa in the early 1990s, dubbed into the Afrikaans language, and entitled 'Rustelose Jare' (Restless Years). In 1999 *The Young and the Restless* was canceled but the show returned to South African television screens in June 2004, with no overhead foreign translations. Episodes are between 11 and 12 months behind that of the USA.

In Sweden, the show aired on tv4 and tv3 from 2002–2005. The show was called *Makt och begär*, which means Power and desire.

In Switzerland, the show airs on TSR at 11:10 as "Les Feux de l'Amour" and is 3 years behind the U.S.

In Turkey, the show used to air on TRT 2. It was called "Yalan Rüzgarı", which means "Wind of Lies" between 1988-1996. The name was derived from the initials of *The Young and the Restless*.

In the Czech Republic *Mladí a neklidní* gets about 2/100 of ranking.

Theme song and other music

Main article: Nadia's Theme

"Nadia's Theme" has been the theme song of *The Young and the Restless* since the show's debut in 1973. The melody, originally titled "Cotton's Dream", was composed by Barry De Vorzon and Perry Botkin, Jr. for the 1971 theatrical film *Bless the Beasts and Children*. The melody was later renamed "Nadia's Theme" after the ABC television network lent the music for Romanian gymnast Nadia Comăneci's performance during the 1976 Summer Olympics.

Botkin wrote a rearranged version of the piece specifically for *The Young and the Restless*' debut. The song remained unchanged, save for a three-year stint in the early 2000s, when an alternate, more jazzy arrangement of that tune was used.

Title sequence

The opening title sequence has also become well-known. For many years since the show's debut, it showcased the characters, drawn by an artist, on a white background. For the first year, the character's portraits were seen behind the *The Young and the Restless* title. For the remaining years until 1984, the characters' headshots were seen to the right of the show's title.

Starting in 1984, the sequence both began and ended with an interlocking Y and R painted on the white canvas in a sweeping brush motion. The logo (and in the earlier years, the drawings) were done by artist Sandy Dvore. The drawings were now sketched with a lighter shade of gray than the previous sketches. The drawings were replaced with live-action shots of the characters in formal or semi-formal wear, still on a white background, in 1988.

Beginning on December 24, 1999, in an unprecedented move for a main title sequence of a daytime soap opera, the names of the principal cast members were mentioned (whereas previously the main title only showed the cast members' faces); however, *Y&R* continues to include the main cast members' names in an alternate version of the closing credits once a week. In 2005, *The Bold and the Beautiful* began showing the performers' names in the title sequence, the only other American soap to do so until February 23, 2010, when *General Hospital* began using the contract cast members' names in the title sequence. The 1999 version also included live-action shots of the characters, but featured in front of a wind blowing satin red curtain as the background.

On March 31, 2003 the title sequence was given a complete makeover, now featuring black-and-white footage from the series with the actors' names in lower case in red at either the top or bottom of the screen (a possible throwback to the shows early years when the cast members sketches were also black and white). Before and after the footage of the actors is the silhouette of a woman in a form-fitting dress walking toward the camera, shown from the neck down. Although the producers have never confirmed the woman's identity, cast member Michelle Stafford (Phyllis) has admitted to being the woman in question. The opening was last updated to reflect new additions to the cast in June 2006. In an interview in December 2008, co-executive producer Maria Arena Bell stated that updating the opening is "on our minds, for sure. We're hopeful we can get to that very soon."

For over 25 years, the announcer for the show's opening and closing credits was Bern Bennett, who would tell viewers to "Join us again for *The Young and the Restless*." In 2003, Bennett retired and CBS hired former casting assistant Marnie Saitta for the job of announcer. In 2006 Marnie Saitta was replaced by cast members announcing for the show.

Closing title

Since the very first episode in 1973, the end credits were always featured on the left side of the screen while the right side consisted of art drawings (1973–1984), the familiar brush stroke logo (1984–1994; 1999–), and the live action cast montage (1994–1999) on the right side of the screen. A longer cut from "Nadia's Theme" was played over the closing, along with the aforementioned announcement "Join us again for *The Young and the Restless*". As with all daytime soaps until the late 1990s, the cast and crew were not credited in every episode; sometimes, the only thing featured in the credits was the copyright info with the production companies listed and the fact the show was taped at CBS Television City. In 1999, CBS did away with the classic closing in favor of inserting a network promo with the credits listed on the network billboard at the bottom of the screen (the right side from 1999–2005); this is a procedure that has become standard among most channels. However, most international networks and SoapNet in the U.S. still broadcast the traditional closing credits.

Ratings

As of 2010, *The Young and the Restless* has managed over 1,000 consecutive weeks in the #1 spot for daytime dramas . Despite this, the show reached a record low of 4,380,000 viewers on Friday, June 13, 2008. Other lows were 4,392,000 viewers on Friday, October 17, 2008, 4,487,000 viewers on Friday, September 19, 2008, 4,491,000 viewers on Friday, May 9, 2008, 4,548,000 on Thursday, October 16, 2008, 4,563,000 viewers on Friday, October 3, 2008, and 4,805,000 viewers on Friday, August 31, 2007.[citation needed]

When introduced during the 1972–73 season, the show was at the bottom of the ratings, but rose rapidly: ninth by 1974–75 and third by 1975–76. By 1988–1989 it had dethroned long-time leader *General Hospital* as the top-rated soap, a position it has held ever since.

Main article: List of US daytime soap opera ratings

Daytime History: Highest Rated Week (November 16–20, 1981) (Nielsen Media Research)

Serial	Household Rating	(Time Slot) Network
General Hospital	16.0	(3-4pm) ABC
All My Children	10.2	(1-2pm) ABC
One Life to Live	10.2	(2-3pm) ABC
Guiding Light	7.9	(3-4pm) CBS
The Young and the Restless	7.3	(11:00–12:00pm) CBS

1995 Daytime Serial Ratings

Rank/Serial	Avg. Millions Of Viewers (Per Episode)
The Young and the Restless	7.155
All My Children	5.891
General Hospital	5.343
The Bold and the Beautiful	5.247
One Life to Live	5.152

Before *The Young and the Restless* was #1

1972-1973 season

- 1. *As the World Turns* 10.6
- 15. *The Young and the Restless* 5.0 (Debut)

1973-1974 season

- 1. *As the World Turns* 10.6 (Tied with Days of our Lives and Another World)
- 13. *The Young and the Restless* 6.2

1974-1975 season

- 1. *As the World Turns* 10.8
- 9. *The Young and the Restless* 8.4

1975-1976 season

- 1. *As the World Turns* 9.4
- 3. *The Young and the Restless* 8.6

1976-1977 season

- 1. *As the World Turns* 9.9
- 4. *The Young and the Restless* 8.7

1977-1978 season

- 1. *As the World Turns* 8.6 (Tied with Another World)
- 5. *The Young and the Restless* 7.8

1978-1979 season

- 1. *All My Children* 9.0
- 3. *The Young and the Restless* 8.6

1979-1980 season

- 1. *General Hospital* 9.9
- 3. *The Young and the Restless* 8.8

1980-1981 season

- 1. *General Hospital* 11.4
- 6. *The Young and the Restless* 7.8

1981-1982 season

- 1. *General Hospital* 11.2
- 5. *The Young and the Restless* 7.4

1982-1983 season

- 1. *General Hospital* 9.8
- 4. *The Young and the Restless* 8.0

1983-1984 season

- 1. *General Hospital* 10.0
- 3. *The Young and the Restless* 8.8

1984-1985 season

- 1. *General Hospital* 9.1
- 3. *The Young and the Restless* 8.1

1985-1986 season

- 1. *General Hospital* 9.2
- 2. *The Young and the Restless* 8.3

1986-1987 season

- 1. *General Hospital* 8.3
- 2. *The Young and the Restless* 8.0

1987-1988 season

- 1. *The Young and the Restless* 8.1 (#1 in Viewers)
- 1. *General Hospital* 8.1

See also

- List of *The Young and the Restless* cast members
- List of *The Young and the Restless* characters
- The children of *The Young and the Restless*
- Minor characters of *The Young and the Restless*
- List of longest-serving soap opera actors
- CBS Daytime

External links

- Official website [2]
- *The Young and the Restless* [3] at CBS Daytime
- *The Young and the Restless* [4] at the Internet Movie Database
- *The Young and the Restless Daily Recaps* [5]
- *The Young and the Restless* [6] at SOAPnet.com
- *The Young and the Restless* [7] at Yahoo! TV [8]
- *The Young and the Restless* [9] at the W. Channel
- Full episodes of *The Young and the Restless* [10] Available only to U.S. viewers
- In depth audio interview with Eric Braeden (Dec 2007) [11]
- *The Young and the Restless* Official Fan Wiki [12] at CBS Wiki

List of Characters

List of The Young and the Restless characters

This is a list of major characters that appear (or have appeared) on the soap opera *The Young and the Restless*.

Contents: Top · 0–9 · A B C D E F G H I J K L M N O P Q R S T U V W X Y Z

A

Ashley Abbott

(Eileen Davidson, 1982-1988, 1999-2007, 2008-present; Brenda Epperson Doumani, 1988-1995; Shari Shattuck, 1996-1999)

Grew up believing John Abbott was her biological father when she's actually the daughter of Brent Davis who had an affair with her mother Dina Mergeron. Mother of Abby Carlton. Suffered a few mental breakdowns.

Jill Foster Abbott

(Brenda Dickson, 1973-1980, 1983-1987; Bond Gideon, 1980; Deborah Adair, 1980-1983, 1986; Jess Walton, 1987-present)

Grew up believing she was the daughter of Bill and Liz Foster until it was learn she was adopted. Mother of Phillip Chancellor III and Billy Abbott. Adopted mother of Cane Ashby. Daughter of Neil Fenmore. Half-sister of Lauren Fenmore Baldwin.

John Abbott (deceased)

(Brett Halsey, 1980-1981; Jerry Douglas, 1982-2006, 2006-2009, 2010)

Father of Jack, Traci, and Billy Abbott. Legal father of Ashley Abbott. Founder and CEO of Jabot Cosmetics. Married and Divorced Jill Foster Abbott twice.

Jack Abbott

(Terry Lester, 1980-1989; Peter Bergman, 1989-present)

Eldest son of John Abbott and Dina Mergeron. Father of Keemo Volien Abbott and Kyle Jenkins. Longtime enemy of Victor Newman.

Keemo Volien Abbott

(Philip Moon, 1994-1996)

Son of Jack Abbott and Luan Volien. Left behind in Vietnam as a baby when Luan left the city until 20 years later when he found by Christine Blair and Paul Williams and reunited with Luan and Jack.

Luan Volien Abbott (deceased)

(Elizabeth Sung, 1994-1996)

First and true love of Jack Abbott. Owner of The Saigon Shack restaurant. Died of a terminal illness.

Billy Abbott

(Katrin and Margret Ingimarsdottir, 1993; Brett Sherman, 1993; Shane Silver, 1993-1995; Josh Michael Rose, 1995-1996; Scotty Leavenworth, 1996-1998; David Tom, 1999-2002; Ryan Brown, 2002-2003; Scott Seymour, 2006; Billy Miller, 2008-present)

Playboy and alcoholic son of John Abbott and Jill Foster Abbott. Father of Cordelia Abbott. Currently runs Restless Style Magazine.

Hope Adams (deceased)

(Signy Coleman, 1993-1995, 1996-1997, 2000, 2002, 2008, 2010; Beth Toussaint, 2006)

Had no eye sight vision. Mother of Victor Adam Newman, Jr. (Adam Wilson). Died from pancreatic cancer.

Barbara Anderson

(Deidre Hall, 1973-1975)

Ex-fiancée of Brad Eliot. Has a son. Had a miscarriage with Brad Eliot's baby.

Betty Andrews

(Lanna Saunders, 1974-1975)

Wife of Jed Andrews.

Jed Andrews

(Tom Selleck, 1974-1975)

Husband of Betty Andrews. Had an affair with Lorie Brooks.

Alana Anthony

(Amy Gibson, 1985)

Daughter of mob boss Joseph Anthony. Dooped into marrying Tyrone Jackson who worked undercover to bring her father down.

Joseph Anthony (deceased)

(Logan Ramsey, 1984-1985)

>Mob boss. Shot to death by police when he was apprehended.

Dr. Logan Armstrong

(Deanna Russo, 2007)

>Found and Nursed Nicholas Newman back to health after his plane crashed. Briefly dated Brad Carlton. Left to work with Doctors without borders in Malawi.

Cane Ashby

(Daniel Goddard, 2007-present)

>Arrived in town posing as the "real" Phillip Chancellor III as he was really working with the real Phillip. Adopted son of Jill Foster Abbott. Has a bad past in hometown Australia.

Boobsie Caswell Austin

(Joy Garrett, 1983-1985)

>A hooker who posed as Nikki in a porno flick for Tony DiSalvo. Friend of Jazz Jackson. Married and Divorced Douglas Austin.

Colonel Douglas Austin

(Michael Evans, 1980-1981, 1981-1985, 1987-1995)

>Best friend of Victor Newman. Former con-man. Married and Divorced Boobsie Caswell.

B

Lowell "River" Baldwin

(Michael Gross, 2008-2009)

>Father of Michael Baldwin and Eden Gerick. First husband of Gloria Bardwell. On the run for illegal activities in 1968.

Michael Baldwin

(Christian LeBlanc, 1991-1993, 1997-present)

>Genoa City primonant defense lawyer. Son of River Baldwin and Gloria Bardwell. Half-brother of Kevin Fisher and Eden Gerick. Father of Fenmore Baldwin. Imprisoned for 4 years for sexually harrassing Christine Blair and rape.

Alison Bancroft

(Lynn Wood, 1982-1984)

>Mother of Kevin Bancroft. Strongly disapproved of Kevin's relationship with Nikki Newman. Kidnapped Victoria Newman.

Earl Bancroft

(Mark Tapscott, 1982-1983)

> Father of Kevin Bancroft. Husband of Alison Bancroft. Attended college with Alison, Kay Chancellor, and Dina Mergeron.

Kevin Bancroft

(Christopher Holder, 1982-1984)

> Son of Earl and Alison Bancroft. Hired by Victor to romance Nikki Newman who he later married. Once thought to be the father of Victoria Newman.

Lillie Belle Barber

(Norma Donaldson, 1990-1994; Robin Braxton, 1994)

> Mother of Olivia and Drucilla Barber Winters. Had a chaotic relationship with Drucilla during her childhood.

Walter Barber

(Henry G. Sanders, 1990-1991; Bennet Guillory, 1992-1994)

> Father of Olivia and Drucilla Barber Winters. Husband of Lillie Belle Barber.

Gloria Bardwell

(Joan Van Ark, 2004-2005; Judith Chapman, 2005-present)

> Mother of Michael Baldwin and Kevin Fisher. Widow of John Abbott. Now co-owns and runs Gloworm restaurant with hubby Jeff Bardwell.

Jeffrey Bardwell

(Ted Shackelford, 2007-present)

> Conning twin brother of Will Bardwell. Blackmailed Gloria into marrying him.

William Bardwell (deceased)

(Ted Shackelford, 2006-2007)

> Genoa City District Attorney. Twin brother of Jeff Bardwell. Married Gloria Bardwell. Died from a stroke.

Lynne Bassett

(Laura Bryan Birn, 1988-2004)

> Paul Williams' longtime faithful secretary. Had a crush on Paul for several years.

Karen Becker

(Brandi Tucker, 1976-1978)

> Daughter of Ron and Nancy Becker. Was in foster care of Snapper Foster and Chris Brooks.

Nancy Becker

(Cathy Carricaburu, 1976-1978)

> Institutionalized wife of Ron Becker and mother of Karen Becker.

Ron Becker

(Dick DeCoit, 1976-1977)

> Father of Karen Becker. Raped Peggy Brooks.

Chase Benson

(Stephen Gregory, 1988-1991)

> Hired by Jill and Kay to romance Nina Webster. Later became good friends with Nina, Cricket Blair and Danny Romalotti. Worked at Jabot Cosmetics.

Alexander "Blade" Bladeson (deceased)

(Michael Tylo, 1992-1995)

> Photographer for Jabot Cosmetics. Married Ashley Abbott. Twin brother of Rick Bladeson. Died when his car was struck on a railroad.

Rick Bladeson

(Michael Tylo, 1994-1995)

> Evil twin brother of Blade Bladeson. Had an affair with Ashley while posing as Blade.

Christine "Cricket" Blair

(Lauralee Bell, 1983-2001, 2002-2006, 2010)

> Daughter of Jessica Blair. Cousin of Joe Blair. Worked as a model for Jabot Cosmetics before becoming a defense lawyer. Once raped by Derek Stuart. Married Danny Romalotti and Paul Williams.

Joe Blair

(John Denos, 1983-1987)

> Photographer for Jabot Cosmetics. Cousin of Christine Blair.

Sean Bridges

(Christopher Douglas, 2001; David Lee Russek, 2001-2002)

> Dated Jill Foster Abbott. Worked on the Glow by Jabot campaign for Jabot Cosmetics.

Christabel "Chris" Brooks

(Trish Stewart, 1973-1978, 1984; Lynne Topping Richter, 1978-1982)

> Daughter of Stuart and Jennifer Brooks. Married Snapper Foster and gave birth to their daughter Jennifer Elizabeth Foster. Raped by George Curtis. Foster mother of Karen Becker.

Elizabeth "Liz" Foster Brooks (deceased)

(Julianna McCarthy, 1973-1985, 1986, 1993, 2003-2004, 2008, 2010)

>Matriarch of the Foster family. Worked as Kay Chancellor's maid for several years. Suffered a stroke and temporary memory loss after pulling her ailing husband Bill Foster's life-support plug.

Jennifer Brooks (deceased)

(Dorothy Green, 1973-1977)

>Matrarch of the Brooks family. Had an affair with Bruce Henderson producing daughter Lorie while married to Stuart Brooks. First Y&R character to deal with breast cancer.

Lauralee "Lorie" Brooks

(Jaime Lyn Bauer, 1973-1982, 1984, 2002)

>Book Author. Daughter of Bruce Henderson and Jennifer Brooks. Framed for murder by mother-in-law Vanessa Prentiss. Married Lance Prentiss. Used and Dumped Victor Newman.

Leslie Brooks

(Janice Lynde, 1973-1977; Victoria Mallory, 1977-1982, 1984)

>Mother of Brooks Prentiss. Suffered a memory loss breakdown. Married Brad Eliot and Lucas Prentiss. Daughter of Stuart and Jennifer Brooks.

Peggy Brooks

(Pamela Peters Solow, 1973-1981, 1984)

>Youngest daughter of Stuart and Jennifer Brooks. Raped by Ron Becker. Had an affair with her college professor Jack Curtis.

Stuart Brooks (deceased)

(Robert Colbert, 1973-1983)

>Patriarch of the Brooks family. Owner of the Genoa City Chronicle. Married Jennifer Brooks and Liz Foster.

Amanda Browning

(Denice Duff, 2001-2002)

>Mother of Mackenzie Browning. Wife of Ralph Hunnicutt. Blackmailed to leave town by Jill Foster Abbott.

Mackenzie Browning

(Ashley Bashioum, 1999-2002, 2004-2005; Kelly Kruger, 2002-2003; Rachel Kimsey, 2005-2006; Clementine Ford, 2009-2010)

>Daughter of Brock Reynolds and Amanda Browning. Surrogate mother of Charlie and Matilda Ashby. Raped by stepfather Ralph Hunnicutt as a child. Volunteers and helps out

with the homeless.

C

Ramona Caceres

(Gladis Jimenez, 1999-2000, 2002)

Girlfriend of madmad Chet Delancy who lived in the desert. Helped Victor Newman escape from Chet.

Daisy Callahan

(Yvonne Zima, 2009-2010)

Daughter of Tom Fisher and Sheila Carter. Fraternal twin sister of Ryder Callahan. Kidnapped and held Jana Hawkes and Lauren Fenmore hostage with Ryder and Aunt Sarah Smythe.

Ryder Callahan

(Wilson Bethel, 2009-2010)

Son of Tom Fisher and Sheila Carter. Fraternal twin brother of Daisy. Conspired in kidnapping and holding Jana Hawkes and Lauren Fenmore hostage. Had an affair with Jana.

Abigail "Abby" Carlton

(Jack and Jenna Hall, 2000; Morgan and Madison Reinherz, 2000-2003; Amanda and Rachel Pace, 2003; Darcy Rose Byrnes, 2003-2007, 2008; Hayley Erin, 2008-2010; Marcy Rylan, 2010-present)

Daughter of Ashley Abbott and Victor Newman. Product of artificial assemination. Adopted by Brad Carlton.

Bradley "Brad" Carlton (deceased)

(Don Diamont, 1985-1996, 1998-2009)

Father of Colleen Carlton and adopted father of Abby Carlton. Stole a deceased friend's identity. Died after falling into a freezing lake saving Noah Newman.

Colleen Carlton (deceased)

(Ashley, Kelly and Bobby Brown, 1992; Caitlin Taylor and Jessica Jaymes Miley, 1993; Natalie and Victoria McCormick, 1993-1994; Alanna Masterson, 1994-1996; Lyndsy Fonseca, 2001-2004, 2004-2005; Adrianne Leon, 2006-2007; Tammin Sursok, 2007-2009)

Daughter of Brad Carlton and Traci Abbott. Best friends with Lily Winters. Died after accidentally drowning when kidnapped by Patty Williams. Heart was donated to Victor Newman.

Molly Carter

> (Marylin Alex, 1991-1993, 1995)
>
>> Mother of Sheila Carter and Sarah Smythe.

Sheila Carter **(deceased)**

> (Kimberlin Brown, 1990-1992, 1993, 1994, 1995, 2005-2006; Michelle Stafford, 2006-2007)
>
>> Longtime enemy of Lauren Fenmore whom she tried to kill several times. Had a miscarriage with Dr. Scott Grainger Sr. baby. Switched Lauren's son with another baby after birth.

Dr. Wesley Carter

> (Ben Watkins, 2002-2004)
>
>> Psychiatrist. Ex-boyfriend of Drucilla Winters. Ex-fiance of Olivia Winters.

Jerry "Cash" Cashman (deceased)

> (John Gibson, 1980-1982)
>
>> Ran The Bayou strip club. Gambler. Dated Kay Chancellor. Died after being stabbed during a gambling dispute.

Katherine Chancellor

> (Jeanne Cooper, 1973-present)
>
>> Town matriarch. Mother of Brock Reynolds and Tucker McCall. Had a longtime feud with Jill Foster Abbott over the death of her husband Phillip Chancellor Sr. Once believed to had been Jill's biological mother.

Phillip Chancellor II **(deceased)**

> (John Considine, 1973-1974; Donnelly Rhodes, 1974-1975)
>
>> Husband of Katherine Chancellor. Later fathered Phillip Chancellor III with Jill Foster Abbott and married her on his deathbed. Former CEO of Chancellor Industries.

Phillip Chancellor III

> (Dick Billingsley, 1978-1981; Chris Hebert, 1981-1982; Jimmy Keegan, 1983; Thom Bierdz, 1986-1989, 2004, 2009, 2010-present)
>
>> Troubled son of Phillip Chancellor and Jill Foster Abbott. Father of Phillip Chancellor IV. Alcoholic. Faked his death for twenty years to cover the fact that he's gay.

Phillip "Chance" Chancellor IV

> (Andrew Clark Rogers, 1988; Chuckie and Kenny Gravino, 1988-1989; Scott and Shaun Markley, 1991-1993; Courtland Mead, 1993-1995; Alex David Linz, 1995-1996; Nicholas Pappone, 1996-1999; Penn Badgley, 2000-2001; John Driscoll, 2009-2010)

Son of Nina Webster and Phillip Chancellor III. Acknowledged Ryan McNeil as his father. Served time in Iraq fighting the war against terrisism. Faked his death to enter the Witness Protection Program after busting shady cops of the Genoa City police force.

David Chow **(deceased)**

(Vincent Irizarry, 2007-2008)

Bigamist. Gambler. Attempted to kill Nikki Newman after marrying her. Murdered his first three wives to collect their money. Killed in a setup car accident. Real name is Angelo Serafini.

Matt Clark (a.k.a. Carter Mills) **(deceased)**

(Eddie Cibrian, 1994-1996; Russell Lawrence, 2000; Rick Hearst, 2000-2001)

Attended high school with Sharon Newman, Nick Newman, and Amy Wilson. Raped Sharon and Amy. Framed Nick for murder twice. Dated Tricia Dennison.

Brandon Collins

(Paul Walker, 1992-1993)

Young employee who worked for Victor Newman who set him up with his daughter Victoria.

Doris Collins

(Victoria Ann-Lewis, 1994. Karen Hensel, 1994-2003, 2005, 2009)

Mother of Sharon Newman. Involved in a car accident that left her paralyzed from the waist on down resulting in her having to use a wheelchair.

Steve Connolly

(Greg Wrangler, 1992-1996, 2001, 2009)

Briefly worked for Jabot Cosmetics. Married Traci Abbott.

Traci Abbott Connolly

(Beth Maitland, 1982-1996, 1999, 2001-2002, 2006, 2007-present)

Book Author. Daughter of John Abbott and Dina Mergeron. Mother of Colleen Carlton. Suffered low self-esteem and dealt with Bulimia. Dated college professor Tim Sullivan. Twice married and divorced Brad Carlton.

Faren Connor (a.k.a. Michelle Harrington)

(Colleen Casey, 1985-1987; Kerry Leigh Michaels, 1991)

Suffered from amnesia. Previously married Evan Sanderson and gave birth to daughter Betsy. Married Andy Richards. Regained her memory before leaving town.

Kurt Costner

(Leigh McCloskey, 1996-1997)

> Bum who worked on the Chancellor Estate. Rescued Ashley Abbott from muggers. Dated Hope Adams.

Marge Cotrooke (deceased)

(Jeanne Cooper, 1989-1990, 2008, 2009)

> Waitress look-alike of Kay Chancellor who was hired by Clint Radison to conspire in taking over Kay's life and fortune. Later became friends with Kay. Alcoholic. Died in a car accident.

Michael Crawford

(Colby Chester, 1985-1990)

> Genoa City lawyer. Had an affair with Jill Foster Abbott while handling her divorce from John Abbott.

George Curtis

(Anthony Geary, 1973)

> Raped Chris Brooks.

Jack Curtis

(Anthony Herrera, 1975-1977)

> College professor. Husband of Joann Curtis. Pursued an affair with his college student Peggy Brooks whom he was briefly engaged to.

Joann Curtis

(Kay Heberle, 1975-1978)

> Wife of Jack Curtis. Suffered from an eating disorder that led her to being overweight. Had very low self-confidence. Was a brief romantic interest of Kay Chancellor.

D

Rick Daros (deceased)

(Randy Holland, 1983-1984)

> Schizophrenic murderer. Hired by Alison Bancroft to breakup her son Kevin's marriage to Nikki Newman. Dated, kidnapped and attempted to kill Nikki. Killed his first wife.

Brent Davis (deceased)

(Jim McMullan, 1984; Bert Kramer, 1984-1985)

> Golf player professional. Had an affair with Dina Mergeron producing their daughter Ashley Abbott. Dated Katherine Chancellor. Died of a liver ailment.

Gary Dawson

(Ricky Paull Goldin, 1999-2000)

Obsessed stalker of Victoria Newman who worked with her as an advertising agent on her Brash & Sassy campaign. Institutionalized.

Tomas Del Cerro

(Francesco Quinn, 1999-2001)

Book Author who became romantically involved with Nina Webster.

Chet Delancy (deceased)

(Marc Singer, 1999)

Madman who lived in a desert and held Victor captive after his plane crashed. Tried to introduce computer virus. Dated Ramona Caceres. Died after falling off a cliff fighting Victor.

Rafael Delgado

(Carlos Bernard, 1999)

Italian boyfriend of Ashley Abbott. Painter. Briefly dated Victoria Newman. Returned to his hometown Madrid Spain.

Keith Dennison

(Granville Van Dusen, 1996-1998, 1999, 2000, 2001; David Allen Brooks, 1999)

Father of Tricia and Megan Dennison. Dated Jill Foster Abbott. Sold his business company to Newman Enterprises.

Rose DeVille (deceased)

(Darlene Conley, 1979-1980, 1986-1987)

Con woman who ran a modeling agency as an undercover prostitution ring. Stole and sold Nina Webster's first baby on the black market.

Tony DiSalvo (deceased)

(Joseph Taylor, 1982-1983)

Mobster who worked for Pete Walker. Raped Cindy Lake. Almost married Nikki Newman. Shot and killed Cindy Lake. Killed by Jazz Jackson.

Sofia Dupre

(Julia Pace Mitchell, 2010-present)

Engaged to Malcolm Winters. Chief Financial Officer for Tucker McCall and his company Tucker McCall Unlimited.

E

Brad Elliot

(Tom Hallick, 1973-1978)

Mugged before arriving in Genoa City. Ex-fiancé of Barbara Anderson. Neurosurgeon and Psychiatrist. Married and divorced Leslie Brooks. Lost his eyesight for a few months.

Carol Robbins Evans

(Christopher Templeton, 1983-1993)

Faithful secretary for Jabot Cosmetics. Married Skip Evans and adopted their daughter Skylar. Wore a leg brace as a result of a childhood illness.

Skip Evans

(Todd Curtis, 1987-1991)

Photographer for Jabot Cosmetics. Married Carol Robbins. Adopted Skylar Evans.

Skylar Carol Evans

(Melissa Bruseth, 1990)

Daughter of teenager Nan Nolan. Adopted by Skip Evans and Carol Robbins Evans.

F

Ernesto Fautsch

(Karl Bruck, 1974-1982, 1984-1985)

Longtime dear friend of the Brooks family. Piano Teacher to Leslie Brooks and Nikki Newman.

Lauren Fenmore

(Tracey E. Bregman, 1983-1995, 2000, 2001-present)

Daughter of Neil Fenmore and JoAnna Manning. Rebellious as a teenager. Mother of Scotty Grainger, Jr. and Fenmore Baldwin. CEO of Fenmore's Department Stores and Boutique. Killed Sheila Carter and Sarah Smythe.

Neil Fenmore (deceased)

(James Storm, 1983-1986)

CEO of Fenmore's Department Stores before his death. Later discovered to be the biological father of Jill Foster Abbott.

Kevin Fisher

(Greg Rikaart, 2003-present)

Internet computer wiz. Son of Tom Fisher and Gloria Bardwell. Had a hard childhood after being abused by Tom and abandoned by older half-brother Michael Baldwin. Attempted to kill Colleen Carlton and himself on separate occasions. Married Jana Hawkes.

Tom Fisher (deceased)

(Roscoe Born, 2005-2006, 2009)

Abusive lowlife ex-husband of Gloria Bardwell and father of Kevin Fisher, Daisy and Ryder Callahan. Dated Ashley Abbott.

Brian Forbes

(Jay Kerr, 1982-1983)

Worked at Jabot Cosmetics. Had a complicated dating relationship with Ashley Abbott.

Greg Foster

(James Houghton, 1973-1976, 2003; Brian Kerwin, 1976-1977; Wings Hauser, 1977-1981, 2010; Howard McGillin, 1981-1982)

Lawyer. Youngest son of Bill and Liz Foster. First husband of Nikki Newman. Was unlucky in love relationships.

William "Snapper" Foster, Jr.

(William Gray Espy, 1973-1975, 2003; David Hasselhoff, 1975-1982, 2010)

Eldest son of Bill and Liz Foster. Father of Chuckie Roulland and Jennifer Elizabeth Foster. Lover of Sally McGuire before marrying Chris Brooks. Medical doctor.

William "Bill" Foster, Sr. (deceased)

(Charles H. Gray, 1975-1976)

Patriarch of the Foster family. Abandoned his family in the late 1960s due to health illness. Died after his life-support was disconnected by his wife Liz.

G

Eric Garrison

(Brian Matthews, 1983-1985)

Had a previous affair with Dina Mergeron. Broken engagement to Ashley Abbott. Never knew he fathered Julia Newman's baby.

Peter Garrett

(Justin Gorence, 1995-1996, 1997-1998)

Dated Phyllis Summers who used him to make her ex-husband jealous. Dated Sasha Green.

Shawn Garrett (deceased)

(Tom McConnell, 1984; Grant Cramer, 1984-1986)

Obsessed fan of Lauren Fenmore. Caused Lauren marriage to Paul Williams to deterioate. Kidnapped Lauren and buried her alive. Previously killed his mother in a house fire. Shot to death.

Eden Gerick

(Erin Sanders, 2008; Vanessa Marano, 2008-2010)

Daughter of River Baldwin and half-sister of Michael Baldwin. Dated Noah Newman.

James "Jim" Grainger

(John Phillip Law, 1989; John O'Hurley, 1989-1990)

Doctor. Father of Scott Grainger Sr. and Christine Blair. Dated Nikki Newman. Married former love Jessica Blair a few months before her death.

Jessica Blair Grainger (deceased)

(Rebecca Street, 1988-1989)

Had an estranged relationship with daughter Christine Blair before finally making amends. Diagnosed with AIDS after having a blood transfusion. Married John Abbott and Jim Grainger.

Scott Grainger, Jr.

(Jessica and Hannah Gist, 1991-1993; Joseph David Tello, 1993-1994; Gemini Barnett, 1994; Blair Redford, 2005-2006)

Son of Dr. Scott Grainger and Lauren Fenmore. Switched at birth with baby Dylan Fenmore by Sheila Carter.

Scott Grainger, Sr. (deceased)

(Peter Barton, 1988-1993)

Medical Doctor. Father of Scotty Grainger, Jr. Briefly dated Christine Blair before learning they were siblings. Married Lauren Fenmore and Sheila Carter. Died from a terminal illness.

Sasha Green (deceased)

(Tina Arning, 1995-1996, 1997, 2002)

Former co-worker of Phyllis Summers who switched Phyllis' baby paternity tests on behalf of Phyllis. Blackmailed Phyllis for money. Dated Peter Garrett. Died in a fire.

Diego Guittierez

(Diego Serrano, 2001-2002; Greg Vaughan, 2002-2003)

Older Brother of Raul Guittierez. Dated Victoria Newman. Pursued an affair with Sharon Newman. Worked as stableboy for the Newman Ranch.

Raul Guittierez

(David Lago, 1999-2004, 2009)

High school friend of Billy, J.T., Brittany, Rianna, and Mackenzie. Dated all his female high school friends. Diagnosed with diabetes in 2001.

H

Devon Hamilton

(Bryton James, 2004-present)

Son of Yolanda Hamilton. Adopted by Neil Winters and Drucilla Winters. Street boy who lived in a children's home before being adopted by the Winters'.

Tyra Hamilton

(Eva Marcille, 2008-2009)

Younger adopted sister of Yolanda Hamilton. Since age 15 she raised Yolanda's daughter Ana as her own and legally adopted her. Dated Neil Winters. Had an affair with Devon.

Yolanda Hamilton

(Chene Lawson, 2005-2006)

Drug addict mother of Devon and Ana Hamilton. Older sister of Tyra Hamilton. Flirted with Neil Winters.

Cynthia Harris

(Lori Saunders, 1977; Heather Lowe, 1977-1978)

Registered nurse who had a romantic interest in Snapper Foster and later Brad Elliot.

Robert Haskell

(Ryan MacDonald, 1989-1990)

Conspired with Clint Radison in kidnapping Katherine Chancellor. Married to Shirley Haskell. Jailed after being apprehended for kidnapping.

Shirley Haskell

(Ruth Silveira, 1989-1990)

Wife of Robert Haskell who also conspired with Clint Radison in kidnapping Katherine Chancellor. Jailed after being apprehended for kidnapping.

Nathan Hastings (deceased)

(Nathan Purdee, 1984-1992; Randy Brooks, 1992-1993; Adam Lazarre-White, 1994-1996, 2000)

Worked with Paul Williams at his investigation firm. Married Olivia Winters and fathered their son Nate. Had an affair with Keesha Monroe. Formerly a hitman for mobster Joseph Anthony.

Nathaniel "Nate" Hastings

(Shantel and Shenice Buford, 1991-1995; Christopher Pope, 1995; Malcolm Hunter, 1995-1996; Bryant Jones, 1996-2002)

Son of Nathan Hastings and Olivia Winters. Olivia mentioned on November 25, 2008 that Nate is attending medical school.

Jana Hawkes

(Emily O'Brien, 2006-2007, 2007-present)

Married Kevin Fisher. Had a brain tumor that caused her to murder Carmen Mesta and set Kevin and Colleen Carlton up to die. Had an affair with Ryder Callahan.

Jeffrey Todd "J.T." Hellstrom

(Thad Luckinbill, 1999-2010)

Married Victoria Newman. Father of Reed Hellstrom. Attended high school with Billy, Mackenzie, Raul, Brittany, and Rianna. Dated Rianna, Mackenzie, and Colleen Carlton.

Bruce Henderson

(Robert Clarke, 1975; Paul Stevens, 1975-1976)

Had an affair with Jennifer Brooks producing daughter Lorie Brooks. Brother of Liz Foster. Father of Mark and Regina Henderson.

Mark Henderson

(Steve Carlson, 1975-1976)

Son of Bruce Henderson. Engaged to Lorie Brooks before cancelling the wedding upon learning they were half-siblings.

Regina Henderson

(Jodean Russo, 1975-1976)

Daughter of Bruce Henderson and sister of Mark Henderson. Half-sister of Lorie Brooks.

Anita Hodges

(Mitzi Kapture, 2002-2005)

Snide wife of Frederick Hodges and mother of Brittany Hodges. Had a brief affair with J.T. Hellstrom.

Brittany Hodges

(Vanessa Lee Evigan, 1999-2000; Lauren Woodland, 2000-2005)

Part of the Glow by Jabot kids with high school mates Billy, Rianna, Mackenzie, Raul, and J.T. Married Bobby Marsino and gave birth to their son Joshua. Daughter of Frederick and Anita Hodges.

Frederick Hodges

(John H. Martin, 2002-2005)

Wealthy Banker. Father of Brittany Hodges. Married to Anita Hodges. Pursued an affair with Jill Foster Abbott.

Vince Holiday (deceased)

(Alex Rebar, 1979-1980, 1986-1987)

Rose DeVille's sidekick in all of her illegal activities of undercover prostitution and selling babies on the black market. Attempted to rape a young girl name Stephanie.

Ben Hollander

(Billy Warlock, 2007, 2008)

Senate campaign manager for Jack Abbott.

Charles "Cole" Howard

(N.P. Schoch, 1980-1981; J. Eddie Peck, 1993-1999)

Book Author. Son of Eve Howard. Once believed to be the son of Victor Newman. Married Victoria Newman and Ashley Abbott. Had an affair with Nina Webster.

Eve Howard (deceased)

(Margaret Mason, 1980-1983, 1984, 1993)

Former secretary and lover of Victor Newman. Mother of Cole Howard. Attempted to kill Victor Newman and Nikki Newman. Died from complications from Venezuelan encephalitis.

Ralph Hunnicutt

(Angelo Tiffe, 2001, 2002; Daniel Quinn, 2002)

Lowlife abusive husband of Amanda Browning. Raped stepdaughter Mackenzie when she was a child. Forced Amanda to help him burglarize the Chancellor estate.

Adrian Hunter

(Mark Derwin, 1989-1990)

In jail. Murdered George Rawlins. Lover of Cassandra Hall Rawlins and later blackmailed her into marriage.

J

Jazz Jackson

> (Jon St. Elwood, 1983-1986)

>> Hitman for Pete Walker and Tony DiSalvo. Later killed Tony. Worked with Paul Williams and Andy Richards at their investigation firm. Brother of Tyrone Jackson.

Tyrone Jackson

> (Phil Morris, 1984-1986)

>> Law student. Brother of Jazz Jackson. Went undercover as a caucasian man named Robert Tyrone. Married mob boss Joseph Anthony's daughter Alana undercover. Dated Amy Lewis.

Diane Jenkins

> (Alex Donnelley, 1982-1984, 1986, 1996-2001; Susan Walters, 2001-2004, 2010; Maura West, 2010-present)

>> Former model at Jabot Cosmetics. Architech. Ex-lover of Jack Abbott. Married Andy Richards and Victor Newman. Conceived son Kyle Jenkins through artificial assemination.

Alice Johnson

> (Tamara Clatterbuck, 1997-2000, 2003, 2005)

>> Adopted mother of Cassie Newman. Daughter of Millie Johnson. Made numerous of visits to Cassie after losing custody of her.

Mamie Johnson

> (Marguerite Ray, 1980-1990; Veronica Redd, 1990-1995, 1999-2002, 2004)

>> Longtime house maid for the Abbott family. Maternal aunt of Olivia and Drucilla Barber Winters. Pursued a brief affair with John Abbott.

K

Ji Min Kim (deceased)

> (Eric Steinberg, 2006-2007)

>> Secretly bought Jabot Cosmetics. Allergic to dogs. Engaged to Jill Foster Abbott at time of his death. Died from suffocation by a crushed windpipe caused by David Chow.

David Kimble (deceased)

> (Drew Pillsbury, 1986; Michael Corbett, 1986-1991)

>> Murderer. Married Nina Webster for her money. The word "Killer" was carved into his forehead after bad cosmetic surgery. Crushed to death after falling into a trash compactor.

Adrian Korbel

>(Eyal Podell, 2006-2008)

>>College Professor. Book Author. Pursued a relationship with fellow college student Colleen Carlton. Briefly dated Heather Stevens. Brief lover of Amber Moore. Moved to Maine.

L

Dr. Joshua Landers (deceased)

>(Heath Kizzier, 1996-1998)

>>Medical Doctor. Married Nikki Newman. Formerly married to Veronica Landers who he had believed died. Shot to death by psychotic first wife Veronica.

Veronica Landers (deceased)

>(Tracy Lindsey Melchior, 1996-1997; Candice Daly, 1997-1998)

>>First wife of Dr. Joshua Landers. Was believed to had died in the early 1990s. Shot Joshua to death. Attempted to kill Nikki Newman twice. Died after falling on a hay pickfork.

Dr. Steven Lassiter (deceased)

>(Rod Arrants, 1987-1988)

>>Psychiatrist for Ashley Abbott and Leanna Love. Fell in love with and married Ashley. Shot to death by the son of one of his patients.

Angela Laurence

>(Elizabeth Keifer, 1982)

>>Daughter of Robert and Claire Laurence. Resented Robert's romantic relationship with Leslie Brooks and tried to split them up.

Claire Laurence

>(Suzanne Zenor, 1982)

>>Wife of Robert Laurence who was institutionalized after learning Robert planned to divorce her. Later regained her sanity. Mother of Angela Laurence.

Robert Laurence

>(Peter Brown, 1981-1982)

>>Lorie Brooks defense attorney during her trial for the death of Vanessa Prentiss. Pursued a relationship with Leslie Brooks. Married to Claire Laurence and father of Angela.

Amy Peters Lewis

>(Stephanie E. Williams, 1983-1988)

Daughter of Frank Lewis. Dated Tyrone Jackson and Nathan Hastings. Taught Nathan how to read. Worked with Paul Williams and Andy Richards at their investigation firm.

Frank Lewis

(Brock Peters, 1982-1985)

Genoa City Police Commisioner. Father of Amy Lewis. Spent a few weeks in a coma after having a heart attack. Moved to San Diego. Suffered a stroke off-screen.

Leanna Love

(Barbara Crampton, 1987-1993, 1998-2002, 2006, 2007)

Former mental patient of Dr. Steven Lassiter. Was a virgin until succumbing to hubby Victor. Wrote ex-husband Victor Newman's unauthorized biography. Owned and hosted a talk show.

Robert Lynch (deceased)

(Terrence McNally, 1993-1994)

Abusive husband of April Stevens. Murdered by April after threatening to harm April's daughter Heather.

Suzanne Lynch

(Ellen Weston, 1978-1980)

Ex-wife of Derek Thurston. Has a institutionalized son with Derek named Jaime. Drugged Kay Chancellor with a mind-altering drug. Went temporaily insane when a presumed dead Kay started tormenting her. Stabbed by Kay.

M

Ronan Malloy

(Jeff Branson, 2010-present)

Nina Webster's long-lost missing first son. Works undercover for the FBI. Helped half-brother Chance Chancellor fake his death.

Joanna Manning

(Susan Seaforth Hayes, 1984-1989, 2005, 2006, 2010)

Estranged mother of Lauren Fenmore. Had another daughter with second husband. Pursued love affair with Marc Mergeron.

Lisa Mansfield

(Lynne Harbaugh, 1988-1989)

Psychotic first wife of Brad Carlton. Kidnapped and held Brad captive in a cabin built-in cage for several weeks.

Adrienne Markham

(Lisa Canning, 2004-2005)

Ex-wife of Damon Porter. Briefly dated Malcolm Winters. Returned to Atlanta, GA to make a fresh start with Damon. Lost a son with Damon.

Robert "Bobby" Marsino (deceased)

(John Enos III, 2003-2005)

Bad turned good guy mobster. Owned and ran Marsino's nightclub. Married Brittany Hodges. Father of Joshua Marsino. Had an affair with Nikki Newman. Killed after going into witness protection.

Mari Jo Mason

(Pamela Bach, 1994; Diana Barton, 1994-1996)

Former lover of Blade Bladeson. Dated Jack Abbott and Keemo Volien Abbott. Shot Victor Newman to near death. Attempted to kill Christine Blair.

Tucker McCall

(William Russ, 2009-2010; Stephen Nichols, 2010-present)

Business man. Estranged long lost son of Katherine Chancellor. Dated Jill Foster Abbott. Dates Ashley Abbott. Owner of Tucker McCall Unlimited and Jabot Cosmetics.

Sally McGuire

(Lee Crawford, 1973-1974, 1981-1982)

Ex-lover of Snapper Foster producing illegitimate son Chuckie. Married Pierre Roulland to give son Chuckie a legal last name.

Ryan McNeil (deceased)

(Scott Reeves, 1991-2001)

Worked at Newman Enterprises when falling for young Victoria Newman who he later married. Married Nina Webster and Tricia Dennison. Shot to death by Tricia.

Tricia Dennison McNeil

(Sabryn Genet, 1997-2001)

Daughter of Keith Dennison and older sister of Megan Dennison. Had an affair with Ryan McNeil while he was married and later married him. Went beserk after miscarrying.

Dina Abbott Mergeron

(Marla Adams, 1983-1986, 1991, 1996, 2008)

First wife of John Abbott. Mother of Jack, Ashley, and Traci Abbott. Walked out on her family in the early 1970s and resurfaced years later after remarrying.

Marc Mergeron

(Frank M. Bernard, 1984, 1987-1988)

Stepson of Dina Mergeron. Dated Ashley Abbott. Lover of JoAnna Manning.

Carmen Mesta (deceased)

(Marisa Ramirez, 2006, 2007)

PR woman for Jabot Cosmetics. Previously had an affair with married bigamist David Chow. Had an affair with Neil Winters. Killed by Jana Hawkes.

Matt Miller

(Robert Parucha, 1985-1987, 2003)

Younger brother of Victor Newman. Dated Ashley Abbott, Nikki Newman, and Casey Reed.

Rianna Miner

(Rianna Loving, 1999-2000; Alexis Thorpe, 2000-2002)

High school friend of Brittany Hodges, Raul Guitterez, Mackenzie Browning, and Billy Abbott. Dated Raul and J.T. Hellstrom.

Chloe Mitchell (a.k.a. Kate Valentine)

(Darla and Sandra Greer, 1990-1991; Danielle Ryah, 1994; Elizabeth Hendrickson, 2008-present)

Daughter of Esther Valentine. Fashion Consultant. Married Cane Ashby after lying saying he fathered her child. Had a complicated relationship with Billy Abbott.

Amber Moore

(Adrienne Frantz, 2006-2010)

Good hearted gold digger. Best friends with Kevin Fisher and Jana Hawkes. Dated and married Daniel Romalotti. Blackmailed by ex-lover Deacon Sharpe. Returned to Los Angeles.

Alec Moretti

(Andre Khabbazi, 1997-1998)

Boyfriend of Megan Dennison. Left town after Megan dumped him for Tony Viscardi.

Estella Munoz

(Anne Betancourt, 2008-2009)

Faithful house manager and servant for the Newman ranch. Left town after being accused of stalking Ashley Abbott.

Patrick Murphy

(Michael Fairman, 2008-present)

Current husband of Katherine Chancellor. Longtime friend of Marge Cotrooke. Loves to play gin and go fishing.

N

Cassie Newman (deceased)

(Camryn Grimes, 1997-2005; 2006; 2007; 2009; 2010)

Sharon Newman's daughter who was given up for adoption and reunited with her seven years later. Died as a young teenager after trying a drunken Daniel Romalotti home.

Julia Newman

(Meg Bennett, 1980-1981; 1982-1984; 1986-1987; 2002)

First wife of Victor Newman and remains good friends with him. Had a daughter by an unaware Eric Garrison.

Nicholas Newman

(Marco and Stefan Flores, 1989; Griffin Ledner, 1990-1991; John Nelson-Alden, 1991-1994; Joshua Morrow, 1994-present)

Son of Victor and Nikki Newman. Framed for murder twice by former classmate Matt Clarke. Married Sharon Collins Newman and Phyllis Summers. Father of Noah, Summer, and Faith Newman. Adopted father of Cassie Newman.

Nikki Newman

(Erica Hope, 1978-1979; Melody Thomas Scott, 1979-present)

Matriarch of the Newman family. Raped by her father Nick Reed. Younger sister of Casey Reed. Recovering Alcoholic. Addicted to pain killers. Involved in several charities.

Noah Newman

(Samantha & Zachary Elkins, 1997; Lauren Summer Harvey, 1997; Hunter Preisendorfer, 1997, 1999-2000; C.J. Hunter, 1998-1999; Nicholas Graziano, 1999; Blake Michael Bryan, 2000-2001; McKay Giller, 2001-2004; Blake Woodruff, 2004; Chase Ellison, 2005; Hunter Allan, 2005-2008; Kevin Schmidt, 2008-2010; Luke Kleintank, 2010-present)

Son of Nicholas and Sharon Newman. Born prematurely. Caught in Clear Springs Parking Garage collision causing him to have his spleen removed. Dated Eden Gerick.

Phyllis Summers Newman

(Michelle Stafford, 1994-1997, 2000-present; Sandra Nelson, 1997-1999)

> Fierce mother of Daniel Romalotti and Summer Newman. Married Danny Romalotti after becoming pregnant with Daniel. Tried to kill Paul Williams and Christine Blair.

Sabrina Costelana Newman (deceased)

(Raya Meddine, 2008; 2009)

> Victoria's best friend from Italy. Fell in love with and married Victor Newman. Killed in a car accident after catching a ride with evil David Chow. Her baby died in the womb.

Sharon Newman

(Monica Potter, 1994; Heidi Mark, 1994; Sharon Case, 1994-present)

> Only daughter of Doris Collins. Mother of Noah Newman and Faith Newman. Married Nick Newman, Jack Abbott, and Adam Newman. Gave daughter Cassie Newman up for adoption after birth and reunited with her seven years later. Raped by Matt Clarke.

Victor Newman

(Eric Braeden, 1980-2009, 2010-present)

> Ruthless business man. Married 9 times to 7 different women. Founder and CEO of Newman Enterprises. Father of Victoria, Nicholas, Adam, and Abby Newman.

Victoria Newman

(Ashley Nicole Millan, 1982-1990; Heather Tom, 1991-1997, 1997-2003; Sarah Aldrich, 1997; Amelia Heinle, 2005-present)

> Eldest child of Victor and Nikki Newman. Mother of Reed Hellstrom. Suffered 3 miscarriages. Worked closely with Victor in different positions at Newman Enterprises.

Nancy "Nan" Nolan

(Mary Sheldon, 1989-1990)

> Teenager who gave her baby Skylar up for adoption to Skip Evans and Carol Robbins Evans.

Brittany Norman

(Melissa Morgan, 1988-1990)

> Auditor for the FBI. Niece of George Rawlins. Had feelings for Paul Williams.

P

Christian Page

>(Vincent Van Patten, 2000)

>>Friend and boyfriend of Ashley Abbott. Labeled as Ashley's baby's father during her pregnancy.

Alex Perez

>(Alexia Robinson, 2000-2002)

>>Broken engagement to Malcolm Winters. Had an affair with Neil Winters. Left town after Malcolm's presumed death.

Dr. Emily Peterson

>(Stacy Haiduk, 2009-2010)

>>Patty's psychiatrist. Identity was stolen by Patty. Relationship with Jack Abbott was messed up due to Patty's interference. Nearly killed by Patty. Institutionalized after being drugged by Patty who had switched places with her.

Damon Porter ·

>(Keith Hamilton Cobb, 2003-2005)

>>Chemist for Jabot Cosmetics. Dated Phyllis Summers. Son Elias was killed at the age of 8. Attempted to kill his son Elias' killer. Moved back to Atlanta with his love Adrienne.

Sam Powers

>(Barry Cahill, 1974-1975)

>>Boyfriend of Liz Foster.

Lance Prentiss

>(John McCook, 1976-1980; Dennis Cole, 1981-1982)

>>Eldest son of Vanessa Prentiss and brother of Lucas Prentiss. Father of Brooks Prentiss. Married Lorie Brooks. Dated Leslie Brooks. CEO of Prentiss Enterprises.

Lucas Prentiss

>(Tom Ligon, 1977-1982)

>>Youngest son of Vanessa Prentiss. Reunited with his family after being found by Lorie Brooks. Previously caused a house fire that disfigured his mother's face.

Vanessa Prentiss (deceased)

>(K. T. Stevens, 1976-1981)

>>Mother of Lance and Lucas Prentiss. Strongly disapproved of Lance's relationship with Lorie Brooks. Wore a veil on lower part of face to hide scars from a house fire. Framed

Lorie for her murder.

R

Clint Radison (deceased)

(Sal Landi, 1988-1989; James Michael Gregary, 1989-1990, 1990-1991, 2009)

Former prison mate of Rex Sterling. Conspired in kidnapping Katherine Chancellor and Esther Valentine and holding them captive. Married Gina Roma. Escaped Jail.

Felipe Ramirez

(Victor Mohica, 1980-1981)

Fisherman who fished Katherine Chancellor out of the sea after she went missing. Was on the run for an attempted assassination of a political figure.

Cassandra Hall Rawlins (deceased)

(Nina Arvesen, 1988-1991)

Wife of wealthy George Rawlins. Suspect of George's mysterious murder. Fell in love with Paul Williams. Married Brad Carlton. Killed when strucked by a car.

George Rawlins (deceased)

(Jonathan Farwell, 1988-1989)

Wealthy businessman. Tried to frame Paul Williams for murder after learning about his affair with Cassandra. Mysteriously murdered by Cassandra's lover Adrian Hunter.

Dr. Casey Reed

(Roberta Leighton, 1978-1981, 1984, 1985-1989, 1998)

Medical doctor. Older sister of Nikki Newman. Dated Brock Reynolds, Greg Foster, Snapper Foster, Lucas Prentiss, and Matt Miller. Raped by father Nick as a child. Stalked by a man named Edward.

Nicholas Reed (deceased)

(Quinn Redeker, 1979)

Rapist father of Casey and Nikki Reed. Killed by daughter Nikki who hit him over the head with a lamp when trying to rape her.

Dr. Tim Reid

(Aaron Lustig, 1996-1997, 2002)

Phyllis' therapist. Fell in love with and dated Phyllis during her separation from Danny Romalotti.

Brock Reynolds

(Beau Kazer, 1974-1980, 1984-1986, 1990-1992, 1999-2003, 2004, 2008, 2009, 2010)

> Beloved son of Katherine Chancellor. Father of Mackenzie Browning. Returned to Kay's life as a changed man who had found God and a new life with the World Hunger Organization, ministering to the disadvantaged people.

Andy Richards

(Steven Ford, 1981-1987, 2002-2003)

> Best friend and business partner of Paul Williams. Dated Nikki Reed. Married Diane Jenkins and Farren Connor. Formerly worked at The Bayou strip nightclub.

Miguel Rodriguez

(Anthony Pena, 1984-2006)

> Longtime housekeeper, servant, and family friend of the Newman family. Had a brief and shaky romance with Veronica Landers.

Callie Rogers

(Michelle Thomas, 1998; Siena Goines, 1998-2000)

> Former girlfriend of Malcolm Winters before later repursuing their former romance. Broke up Malcolm's marriage to Olivia Winters. Nightclub singer.

Gina Roma

(Patty Weaver, 1982-2009)

> Socialite. Daughter of Rex Sterling and sister of Danny Romalotti. Owner and Hostess of her restaurant Gina's before it was burnt down by Kevin Fisher and later The Genoa City Athletic Club.

Daniel Romalotti, Jr.

(Hannah and Desiree Wheelan, 1994-1996; Michael McElroy, 1996-1997; Chase Bebak, 1997-1998; Roland Gibbons, 1998; Cam Gigandet, 2004; Michael Graziadei, 2004-present)

> Son of Phyllis Summers and Brian Hamilton. Legal son of rock-n-roller Danny Romalotti. Married Lily Winters and Amber Moore. Charged for Cassie Newman's death until the truth came out.

Daniel "Danny" Romalotti, Sr.

(Michael Damian, 1981-1993, 1994-1998, 2003-2004, 2008)

> Rock and Roll singer. Son of Rex Sterling and brother of Gina Roma. Married Christine Blair and Phyllis Summers. Dated Patty Williams.

Marianne Roulland

(Lilyan Chauvin, 1974)

> Sister of Pierre Roulland.

Pierre Roulland

> (Robert Clary, 1973-1974)

>> Owner of and singer at his restaurant Pierre's. Married Sally McGuire to give her son Chuckie a legitimate last name. Shot to death when his restaurant was robbed.

Roxanne (Last name unknown)

> (Tatyana Ali, 2007-present)

>> Girlfriend of Devon Hamilton.

S

Jed Sanders

> Josh Taylor (1993-1994)

Evan Sanderson (deceased)

> John Shearin (1986-1987)

Michael Scott

> Nicholas Benedict (1980-1981)

Gwen Sherman

> Jennifer Leak (1974-1975)

John Silva

> John Castellanos (1989-2004)

Dr. Stephanie Simmons

> Vivica A. Fox (1994-1995)

> Angelle Brooks (1996)

Sarah Smythe (**deceased**)

> Tracey E. Bregman (2010)

Rex Sterling (deceased)

> Quinn Redeker (1987-1994, 2004)

April Stevens

> Janet Wood (1979)

> Cynthia Eilbacher (1979-1982, 1992-1994)

> Rebecca Staub (2008)

Heather Stevens

> Dana and Lauren Schankman (1979)

Claire and Elizabeth Schoene (1979-1982)

Conci Nelson (1993-1994)

Vail Bloom (2007-2010)

Eden Riegel (2010-present)

Derek Stuart (deceased)

Ken Olandt (1989)

Professor Tim Sullivan

Scott Palmer (1983-1987, 1988-1989)

T

Karen Taylor

Nia Peeples (2007-2009)

Joseph Thomas

Quinn Redeker (1979-1980)

Derek Thurston

Caleb Stoddard (1976)

Jeff Cooper (1976)

Joe LaDue (1977-1981, 1984)

Rafe Torres

Yani Gellman (2008-present)

Grace Turner

Josie Davis (1996-1997)

Jennifer Gareis (1997-1999, 2000, 2001, 2002, 2004)

V

Esther Valentine

Kate Linder (1982-present)

Antonio "Tony" Viscardi (deceased)

Nick Scotti (1996-1999)

Jay Bontatibus (1999-2000)

Megan Dennison Viscardi

Ashley Jones (1997-2000, 2001)

W

Pete Walker (deceased)

William Bassett (1982-1983)

Larry Warton

David "Shark" Fralick (1995-1996, 1999-2004, 2005)

Florence "Flo" Webster

Sharon Farrell (1991-1996)

Nina Webster

Tricia Cast (1986-2001, 2008, 2009-present)

Lindsey Wells

Lauren Koslow (1984-1986)

Diane Wenstin

Devon Pierce (1990-1991)

Roger Wilkes

David Leisure (2009)

Annie Wilkes

Marcia Wallace (2009)

Carl Williams

Brett Hadley (1980-1990, 1998-1999)

Isabella Braña Williams

Eva Longoria Parker (2001-2003)

Mary Williams

Carolyn Conwell (1980-2004)

Patty Williams (a.k.a. Mary Jane Benson)

Tammy Taylor (1980)

Lilibet Stern (1980-1983)

Andrea Evans (1983-1984)

Stacy Haiduk (2009-2010)

Paul Williams

Doug Davidson (1978-present)

Steven Williams

David Winn (1980-1981)

Amy Wilson

>   Robin Scott (1994)

>   Julianne Morris (1994-1996)

Cliff Wilson (deceased)

>   David Cowgill (1993-1996)

Judy Wilson

>   Loyita Chapel (1980-1981)

Adam Wilson

>   Celeste and Coryn Williams (1995)

>   Danielle and Sabrina Hepler (1995)

>   Spencer Klass (1995-1996)

>   Hayden Tank (1996-1997, 2002)

>   Chris Engen (2008-2009)

>   Michael Muhney (2009-present)

Ellen Winters

>   Jennifer Karr (1986-1987)

Drucilla Winters **(presumed deceased)**

>   Victoria Rowell (1990-1998, 2000, 2002-2007)

Keesha Monroe Winters (deceased)

>   Wanda Acuna (1994-1995)

>   Jennifer Gatti (1995-1996)

Lily Winters

>   Vanessa Carlson (1995-1996)

>   Brooke Marie Bridges (1996-1998, 2000)

>   Christel Khalil (2002-2005, 2006-present)

>   Davetta Sherwood (2006)

Malcolm Winters

>   Shemar Moore (1994-2002, 2004-2005)

>   Darius McCrary (2009-present)

Neil Winters

>   Kristoff St. John (1991-present)

Dr. Olivia Winters

Tonya Lee Williams (1990-2005, 2007, 2008-present)

List of Cast Members

List of The Young and the Restless cast members

Current cast members

Actor	Character	Duration
Peter Bergman	Jack Abbott (#2)	1989–
Eric Braeden	Victor Newman	1980–2009, 2010–
Jeff Branson	Ronan Malloy	2010–
Sharon Case	Sharon Newman (#2)	1994–
Judith Chapman	Gloria Bardwell (#2)	2005–
Jeanne Cooper	Katherine Chancellor	1973–
Doug Davidson	Paul Williams	1978–
Eileen Davidson	Ashley Abbott (#1)	1982–1988, 1999–2007, 2008–
Daniel Goddard	Cane Ashby	2007–
Michael Graziadei	Daniel Romalotti	2004–
Amelia Heinle	Victoria Newman Abbott (#3)	2005–
Elizabeth Hendrickson	Chloe Mitchell	2008–
Bryton James	Devon Hamilton	2004–
Christel Khalil	Lily Ashby (#1)	2002–2005, 2006–
Christian LeBlanc	Michael Baldwin	1991–1993, 1997–
Kate Linder	Esther Valentine	1982–
Darius McCrary	Malcolm Winters (#2)	2009 –
Billy Miller	Billy Abbott (#4)	2008–
Julia Pace Mitchell	Sofia Dupre	2010-
Joshua Morrow	Nicholas Newman	1994–
Michael Muhney	Adam Newman (#2)	2009–

Stephen Nichols	Tucker McCall (#2)	2010–
Emily O'Brien	Jana Hawkes	2006–
Eden Riegel	Heather Stevens (#2)	2010–
Greg Rikaart	Kevin Fisher	2003–
Marcy Rylan	Abby Newman (#2)	2010–
Melody Thomas Scott	Nikki Newman (#2)	1979–
Kristoff St. John	Neil Winters	1991–
Michelle Stafford	Phyllis Summers Newman (#1)	1994–1997, 2000–
Jess Walton	Jill Abbott Fenmore (#4)	1987–
Maura West	Diane Jenkins (#3)	2010–

Recurring cast members

Actor	Character	Duration
Tatyana Ali	Roxanne	2007–
Michael Badalucco	Hogan	2010–
Samantha Bailey	Summer Newman	2009–
Thom Bierdz	Phillip Chancellor III	1986–1989, 2004, 2009, 2010–
Tracey E Bregman	Lauren Fenmore Baldwin	1983–1995, 2000, 2001–
Tricia Cast	Nina Webster	1986–2001, 2008, 2009–
Michael Fairman	Patrick Murphy	2008–
Yani Gellman	Rafe Torres	2008–
Sean Kanan	Deacon Sharpe	2009–2010, 2010–
Luke Kleintank	Noah Newman	2010–
Paul Leyden	Blake Whitcomb	2010–
Beth Maitland	Traci Abbott Connolly	1982–1996, 1999, 2001–2002, 2006, 2007–
Eric Roberts	Vance Abrams (#2)	2010–
Garrett Ryan	Kyle Jenkins	2010–
Ted Shackelford	Jeffrey Bardwell	2007–

Laura Stone	Skye Newman	2008, 2010–
Sean Young	Meggie McClaine	2010–

Upcoming cast members

Actor	Character	Status
Thad Luckinbill	J.T. Hellstrom	Exits November 5
Clementine Ford	Mackenzie Browning (#4)	Exits November 5

Former cast members

Actor	Character	Duration
Robert Ackerman	John Harding #1	1981
Wanda Acuna	Keesha Monroe #1	1995
Deborah Adair	Jill Foster Abbott #3	1980–1983, 1986
Marla Adams	Dina Mergeron	1983–1986, 1991, 1996, 2008
Josh Albee	Tony Baker	1979–1980
Sarah Aldrich	Victoria Newman #3	1997
Marilyn Alex	Molly Carter	1991–1993, 1995
Hunter Allan	Noah Newman	2005–2008
Beverly Archer	Shirley Sherwood	1999
Tina Arning	Sasha Green	1995–1996, 1997, 2002
Rod Arrants	Steven Lassiter	1987–1988
Nina Arvesen	Cassandra Hall Rawlins	1988–1991
Linden Ashby	Cameron Kirsten	2003–2004
Pamela Bach	Mari Jo Mason #1	1994
Penn Badgley	Phillip Chancellor IV #8	2000–2001
Diana Barton	Mari Jo Mason #2	1994–1996
Peter Barton	Scott Grainger Sr.	1988–1993
Ashley Bashioum	Mackenzie Browning #1	1999–2002, 2004–2005
William Bassett	Pete Walker	1982–1983

Jaime Lyn Bauer	Lorie Brooks	1973–1982, 1984, 2002
Fred Beir	Mitchell Sherman #1	1975–1985
Lauralee Bell	Christine Blair	1983–2001, 2002–2006, 2010
Nicholas Benedict	Michael Scott	1980–1981
Meg Bennett	Julia Newman	1980–1981, 1982–1984, 1986–1987, 2002
Carlos Bernard	Rafael Delgado	1999
Frank M. Bernard	Marc Mergeron	1984, 1987–1988
Wilson Bethel	Ryder Callahan	2009–2010
Leslie Bevis	Ruth Perkins	1998–1999
Dick Billingsley	Phillip Chancellor III #1	1978–1981
Laura Bryan Birn	Lynne Bassett	1988–2004
Vail Bloom	Heather Stevens	2007–2010
Vasili Bogazianos	Al Fenton	1998–1999
Jay Bontatibus	Tony Viscardi #2	1999–2000
Roscoe Born	Tom Fisher	2005–2006, 2009
Kimberlin Brown	Sheila Carter #1	1990–1992, 1993, 1994, 1995, 2005–2006
Peter Brown	Robert Laurence	1981–1982
Ryan Brown	Billy Abbott	2002–2003
Karl Bruck	Maestro Faustch	1974–1982, 1984–1985
Darcy Rose Byrnes	Abby Carlton	2003–2007, 2008
Barry Cahill	Sam Powers #2	1974–1975
Lisa Canning	Adrienne Markham	2004–2005
Cathy Carricaburu	Nancy Becker	1976–1978
Colleen Casey	Faren Connor #1	1985–1987
John Cassidine	Phillip Chancellor II #1	1973–1974
John Castellanos	John Silva	1989–1998, 1998–2004
Loyita Chapel	Judy Wilson	1980–1981
Colby Chester	Michael Crawford	1985–1990
Eddie Cibrian	Matt Clark #1	1994–1996
Robert Clary	Pierre Roulland	1973–1974
Tamara Clatterbuck	Alice Johnson	1997–1999, 2000, 2003, 2005
Keith Hamilton Cobb	Damon Porter	2003–2005

Robert Colbert	Stuart Brooks	1973–1983
Dennis Cole	Lance Prentiss #2	1981–1982
Signy Coleman	Hope Adams	1993–1995, 1996–1997, 2000, 2002, 2008, 2010
Darlene Conley	Rose DeVille	1979–1980, 1986–1987
Carolyn Conwell	Marion Reeves Mary Williams	1977 1980–2004
Jeff Cooper	Derek Thurston #2	1976
Michael Corbett	David Kimble #2	1986–1991
Melinda Cordell	Dorothy Stevens Madame Estelle Chavin	1980–1982, 1993 1990–1994
Grant Cramer	Shawn Garrett #2	1984–1986
Barbara Crampton	Leanna Love	1987–1993, 1998, 1999, 2000–2001, 2002, 2006, 2007
Lee Crawford	Sally McGuire	1973–1974, 1981–1982
Todd Curtis	Skip Evans	1987–1991
Linwood Dalton	Jared Markson	1984–1985
Candice Daly	Veronica Landers #2	1997–1998
Michael Damian	Danny Romalotti	1981–1993, 1994–1998, 2002, 2003–2004, 2008
Edgar Daniels	Sebastian Crown	1980
Josie Davis	Grace Turner #1	1996–1997
Marita De Leon	Joani Garza	1995–1998
Lee Debroux	John Harding #2	1981
Dick DeCoit	Ron Becker	1976–1977
John Denos	Joe Blair	1983–1987
Mark Derwin	Adrian Hunter	1989–1990
Don Diamont	Brad Carlton	1985–1996, 1998–2009
Brenda Dickson	Jill Foster Abbott #1	1973–1980, 1983–1987
Norma Donaldson	Lillie Belle Barber	1990–1994
Alex Donnelley	Diane Jenkins #1	1982–1984, 1986, 1996–2001
Christopher Douglas	Sean Bridges #1	2001
Jerry Douglas	John Abbott #2 Alistair Wallingford	1982–2006, 2006–2009, 2010 2008
John Driscoll	Phillip "Chance" Chancellor IV #9	2009–2010
Denice Duff	Amanda Browning	2001–2002

Cindy Eilbacher	Jody Conway April Stevens #2	1977 1979–1982, 1992–1994
Chris Engen	Adam Wilson	2008–2009
John Enos III	Bobby Marsino	2003–2005
Brenda Epperson	Ashley Abbott #2	1988–1995
Hayley Erin	Abby Carlton	2008-2010
William Gray Espy	Snapper Foster #1	1973–1975, 2003
Andrea Evans	Patty Williams #3 Tawny Moore	1983–1984 2010
Michael Evans	Col. Douglas Austin	1980–1981, 1981–1985, 1987–1995
Sharon Farrell	Florence Webster	1991–1996
Lyndsy Fonseca	Colleen Carlton	2001–2004, 2004–2005
Steven Ford	Andy Richards	1981–1987, 2002–2003
Vivica A. Fox	Stephanie Simmons	1994–1995
David "Shark" Fralick	Larry Warton	1995–1996, 1999–2004, 2005
Adrienne Frantz	Amber Moore	2006–2010
Jennifer Gareis	Grace Turner #2	1997–1999, 2000, 2001, 2002, 2004
Joy Garrett	Boobsie Caswell Austin	1983–1985
Kelly Garrisson	Rebecca Harper Hilary Lancaster	1990 1991-1993
Jennifer Gatti	Keesha Monroe #2	1995–1996
Anthony Geary	George Curtis	1973
Sabryn Genet	Tricia Dennison McNeil	1997–2001
Amy Gibson	Alana Anthony	1985
John Gibson	Jerry "Cash" Cashman	1980–1982
Bond Gideon	Jill Foster Abbott #2	1980
Siena Goines	Callie Rogers #2	1998–2000
Ricky Paull Goldin	Gary Dawson	1999–2000, 2000
Justin Gorence	Peter Garrett	1995–1996, 1997–1998
Charles H. Gray	Bill Foster	1975–1976
Veleka Gray	Ruby Collins Sharon Reaves	1983 1983–1984
Dorothy Green	Jennifer Brooks	1973–1977

James Michael Gregary	Clint Radison #2	1989–1990, 1990–1991, 2009
Stephen Gregory	Chase Benson	1988–1991
Camryn Grimes	Cassie Newman	1997–2005, 2006, 2007, 2009, 2010
Michael Gross	River Baldwin	2008–2009
Bennet Guillory	Walter Barber #2	1992–1994
Brett Hadley	Carl Williams	1980–1990, 1998–1999
Stacy Haiduk	Patty Williams #4 Dr. Emily Peterson	2009–2010
Deidre Hall	Barbara Anderson	1973–1975
Tom Hallick	Brad Elliot	1973–1978
Brett Halsey	John Abbott #1	1980–1981
Lynne Harbaugh	Lisa Mansfield	1988–1989
David Hasselhoff	Snapper Foster #2	1975–1982, 2010
Wings Hauser	Greg Foster #3	1977–1981, 2010
Susan Seaforth Hayes	JoAnna Manning	1984–1989, 2005, 2006, 2010
Rick Hearst	Matt Clark #3	2000–2001
Kay Heberle	Joann Curtis	1975–1978
Chris Hebert	Phillip Chancellor III #2	1981–1982
Karen Hensel	Doris Collins #2	1994–2003, 2005, 2009
Anthony Herrera	Jack Curtis	1975–1977
Christopher Holder	Kevin Bancroft	1982–1984
Randy Holland	Rick Daros	1983–1984
Erica Hope	Nikki Newman #1	1978–1979
James Houghton	Greg Foster #1	1973–1976, 2003
Vincent Irizarry	David Chow	2007–2008
Gladys Jimenez	Ramona Caceres	1999–2000, 2002
Ashley Jones	Megan Dennison Viscardi	1997–2000, 2001
Bryant Jones	Nate Hastings	1996–2002
James Ivy	Jeremy Ross	1997
Sean Kanan	Deacon Sharpe	2009-2010, 2010
Mitzi Kapture	Anita Hodges	2002–2005
Jennifer Karr	Ellen Winters	1986–1987

Beau Kazer	Brock Reynolds	1974–1980, 1984–1986, 1990–1992, 1999–2004, 2008, 2009, 2010
Jimmy Keegan	Phillip Chancellor III #3	1983
Jay Kerr	Brian Forbes	1982–1983
Brian Kerwin	Greg Foster #2	1976–1977
Andre Khabbazi	Alec Moretti	1997–1998
Rachel Kimsey	Mackenzie Browning #3	2005–2006
Heath Kizzier	Dr. Joshua Landers	1996–1998
Lauren Koslow	Lindsey Wells	1984–1986
Bert Kramer	Brent Davis #2	1984–1985
Kelly Kruger	Mackenzie Browning #2	2002–2003
Jerry Lacy	Jonas	1979–1982
Joe LaDue	Derek Thurston #3	1977–1981, 1984
David Lago	Raul Guittierez	1999–2004, 2009
Sal Landi	Clint Radison #1 Poker Player	1988–1989 2010
Greg Lauren	Brett Nelson	1998–1999
John Phillip Law	Dr. Jim Grainger #1	1989
Russell Lawrence	Matt Clark #2	2000
Chene Lawson	Yolanda Hamilton	2005–2006
Adam Lazarre-White	Nathan Hastings #3	1994–1996, 2000
Jennifer Leak	Gwen Sherman	1974–1975
Roberta Leighton	Casey Reed	1978–1981, 1984, 1985–1989, 1998
Adrianne Leon	Colleen Carlton	2006–2007
Terry Lester	Jack Abbott #1	1980–1989
Victoria Ann Lewis	Doris Collins #1	1994
Tom Ligon	Lucas Prentiss	1977–1982
Eva Longoria	Isabella Braña Williams	2001–2003
William Long, Jr.	Wayne Stevens	1980–1982
Rianna Loving	Rianna Miner #1	1999–2000
Heather Lowe	Cynthia Harris #2	1977–1978
Aaron Lustig	Dr. Tim Reid	1996–1997, 2002
Janice Lynde	Leslie Brooks #1	1973–1977

Ryan MacDonald	Robert Haskell	1989–1990
Victoria Mallory	Leslie Brooks Prentiss #2	1977–1982, 1984
Vanessa Marano	Eden Gerick #2	2008-2010
Eva Marcille	Tyra Hamilton	2008–2009
Heidi Mark	Sharon Newman #2	1994
John H. Martin	Frederick Hodges	2002–2005
Margaret Mason	Eve Howard	1980–1983, 1984, 1993
Brian Matthews	Eric Garrison	1983–1985
Julianna McCarthy	Liz Foster	1973–1985, 1986, 1993, 2003–2004, 2008, 2010
Leigh McCloskey	Kurt Costner	1996–1997
Tom McConnell	Shawn Garrett #1	1984
John McCook	Lance Prentiss #1 Eric Forrester	1976–1980 1993, 2005
Howard McGillin	Greg Foster #4	1981–1982
Dorothy McGuire	Cora Miller	1984
Jim McMullan	Brent Davis #1	1984
Terrence McNally	Robert Lynch	1993–1994
Raya Meddine	Sabrina Costelana	2008, 2009
Tracy Lindsey Melchior	Veronica Landers #1	1997
Ernestine Mercer	Millie Johnson	1997–1999, 2000
Freeman Michaels	Drake Belson	1995–1996
Jeanna Michaels	Karen Richards	1981–1982
Kerry Leigh Michaels	Faren Connor #2 "Michelle Harrington"	1991
Ashley Nicole Millan	Victoria Newman #1	1982–1990
William Mims	Sam Powers #1	1973
Victor Mohica	Felipe Ramirez	1980–1981
Philip Moon	Keemo Volien Abbott	1994–1996
Shemar Moore	Malcolm Winters #1	1994–2002, 2004–2005
Melissa Morgan	Brittany Norman	1988–1990
Julianne Morris	Amy Wilson #2	1994–1996
Phil Morris	Tyrone Jackson	1984–1986

Conci Nelson	Betsy Sanderson	1987
	Heather Stevens	1993–1994
Sandra Nelson	Phyllis Summers Newman #2	1997–1999
Lee Nicholl	Sven Peterson	1985–1986
John O'Hurley	Dr. Jim Grainger #2	1989–1990
Ken Olandt	Derek Stuart	1989
Scott Palmer	Tim Sullivan	1983–1987, 1988–1989
Nicholas Pappone	Phillip Chancellor IV #7	1996–1999
Robert Parucha	Matt Miller	1985–1987, 2003
J. Eddie Peck	Cole Howard	1993–1999
Nia Peeples	Karen Taylor	2007–2009
Anthony Pena	Miguel Rodriguez	1984–2003, 2004, 2005
Brock Peters	Frank Lewis	1982–1985
Devon Pierce	Diane Westin	1990–1991
Drew Pillsbury	David Kimble #1	1986
Eyal Podell	Adrian Korbel	2006–2008
Monica Potter	Sharon Newman #1	1994
Nathan Purdee	Nathan Hastings #1	1984–1992
Daniel Quinn	Ralph Hunnicutt	2002
Francesco Quinn	Tomas Del Cerro	1999–2001
Marisa Ramirez	Carmen Mesta	2006, 2007
	Ines Vargas	2007
Logan Ramsey	Joseph Anthony	1984–1985
Margueritte Ray	Mamie Johnson #1	1980–1990
Alex Rebar	Vince Holliday	1979–1980, 1986–1987
Veronica Redd	Mamie Johnson #2	1990–1995, 1999, 2000, 2001, 2002, 2004
Quinn Redeker	Nicholas Reed	1979
	Joseph Thomas	1979–1980
	Rex Sterling	1987–1994, 2004
Blair Redford	Scott Grainger, Jr.	2005–2006
Marianne Rees	Mai Volien	1994–1996
Scott Reeves	Ryan McNeil	1991–2001
Donnelly Rhodes	Phillip Chancellor II #2	1974–1975

David Richards	Sid Garber	1996–1998, 2000
Lynne Topping Richter	Christabel Brooks #2	1978–1982
Deanna Robbins	Cindy Lake	1982–1983
Alexia Robinson	Alex Perez	2000–2002
Victoria Rowell	Drucilla Winters	1990–1998, 2000, 2002–2007
David Lee Russek	Sean Bridges #2	2001–2002
Deanna Russo	Logan Armstrong	2007
Jodean Russo	Regina Henderson	1975–1976
William Russ	Tucker McCall #1	2009–2010
Erin Sanders	Eden Gerick #1	2008
Henry G. Sanders	Walter Barber #1	1990–1991
Lanna Saunders	Betty Andrews	1974–1975
Lori Saunders	Cynthia Harris #1	1977
Beth Scheffel	Barbara Ann Harding	1981–1982
Kevin Schmidt	Noah Newman	2008–2010
Robin Scott	Amy Wilson #1	1994
Nick Scotti	Tony Viscardi #1	1996–1999
Tom Selleck	Jed Andrews	1974–1975
Diego Serrano	Diego Guittierez #1	2001–2002
Scott Seymour	Billy Abbott	2006
Shari Shattuck	Ashley Abbott #3	1996–1999
John Shearin	Evan Sanderson	1986–1987
Mary Sheldon	Nancy "Nan" Nolan	1989–1990
Davetta Sherwood	Lily Winters Ashby	2006
Ruth Silvera	Shirley Haskell	1989–1990
Marc Singer	Chet Delancy	1999
Asia Ray Smith	Sierra Hoffman	2003–2006
Pamela Peters Solow	Peggy Brooks	1973–1981, 1984
Jon St. Elwood	Jazz Jackson	1983–1986
Jack Stauffer	Scott Adams	1978–1979
Eric Steinberg	Ji Min Kim	2006–2007
Dawn Stern	Vanessa Lerner	2003–2004

Lilibet Stern	Patty Williams #2	1980–1983
K. T. Stevens	Vanessa Prentiss	1976–1981
Paul Stevens	Bruce Henderson #2	1975–1976
Trish Stewart	Christabel Brooks Foster #1	1973–1978, 1984
Caleb Stoddard	Derek Thurston #1	1976
Jim Storm	Neil Fenmore	1983–1986
Rebecca Street	Jessica Blair	1988–1989
Maxine Stuart	Margaret Dugan	1993, 1996
Elizabeth Sung	Luan Volien Abbott	1994–1996
Tammin Sursok	Colleen Carlton	2007–2009
Mark Tapscott	Earl Bancroft	1982–1983
Joseph Taylor	Tony DiSalvo	1982–1983
Josh Taylor	Jed Sanders	1993–1994
Tammy Taylor	Patty Williams #1	1980
Christopher Templeton	Carol Robbins Evans	1983–1993
Michelle Thomas	Callie Rogers #1	1998
Gordon Thomson	Patrick Baker	1997–1998
Alexis Thorpe	Rianna Miner #2	2000–2002
David Tom	Billy Abbott	1999–2002
Heather Tom	Victoria Newman #2	1991–1997, 1997–2003
Brandi Tucker	Karen Becker	1976–1978
Michael Tylo	Blade Bladeson Rick Bladeson	1992–1995 1994–1995
Joan Van Ark	Gloria Bardwell #1	2004–2005
Granville Van Dusen	Keith Dennison #1	1997–1998, 1999, 2000, 2001
Vincent Van Patten	Christian Page	2000
Greg Vaughan	Diego Guittierez #2	2002–2003
Paul Walker	Brandon Collins	1992–1993
Susan Walters	Diane Jenkins #2	2001–2004, 2010
Billy Warlock	Ben Hollander	2007, 2008
Ben Watkins	Wesley Carter	2002–2004
Patty Weaver	Gina Roma	1982–2009

Ellen Weston	Suzanne Lynch	1978–1980
Stephanie E. Williams	Amy Peters Lewis	1983–1988
David Winn	Steven Williams	1980–1981
William Wintersole	Mitchell Sherman #2	1986–1996, 1998, 2003, 2008, 2009
Janet Wood	April Stevens #1	1979
Lynn Wood	Alison Bancroft	1982–1984
Lauren Woodland	Brittany Hodges #2	2000–2005
Greg Wrangler	Steve Connolly	1992–1996, 1999, 2001, 2009
Yvonne Zima	Daisy Callahan	2009–2010

Notable recurring cast members

Actor	Role	Tenure
Linden Ashby	Cameron Kirsten	2003–2004
Penn Badgley	Phillip Chancellor IV	2000–2001
David Hedison	Arthur Hendricks	2004
Brody Hutzler	Cody Dixon	1999–2004
Michael Nouri	Elliott Hampton	2004
Millie Perkins	Rebecca Kaplan	2006
Eric Roberts	Vance Abrams	2010
Ted Shackelford	William Bardwell Jeffrey Bardwell	2006–2007 2007-
Asia Ray Smith	Sierra Hoffman	2003–2006
Kim Strauss	Dr. Reese Walker	1995–2006
Don Swayze	Charlie Shaw	2010
Beth Toussaint	Hope Adams	2006
Sean Young	Meggie Mclaine	2010

Deceased cast members

Actor	Role	Date of death
John Gibson	Jerry "Cash" Cashman	May 17, 1986
Karl Bruck	Maestro Ernesto Faustche	April 21, 1987
Hugh McPhillips	Andre (#4)	October 31, 1990
Joy Garrett	Boobsie Caswell Austin	February 11, 1993
Norma Donaldson	Lillie Belle Barber	November 22, 1994
Michelle Thomas	Callie Rogers	December 23, 1998
Margaret Mason	Eve Howard	March 26, 1999
Logan Ramsey	Joseph Anthony	June 26, 2000
Terry Lester	Jack Abbott (#1)	November 28, 2003
Elizabeth Harrower	Charlotte Ramsey	December 10, 2003
Candice Daly	Veronica Landers (#2)	December 14, 2004
Brock Peters	Frank Lewis	August 23, 2005
Darlene Conley	Rose DeVille	January 14, 2007
Lanna Saunders	Betty Andrews	March 10, 2007
Michael Evans	Col. Douglas Austin	September 4, 2007
Dorothy Green	Jennifer Brooks	May 8, 2008
John Phillip Law	Dr. Jim Grainger (#1)	May 13, 2008
Dennis Cole	Lance Prentiss (#2)	November 15, 2009

Before they were stars

Actor	Role	Tenure
Eddie Cibrian	Matt Clark (#1)	1994–1995
Thomas Dekker	Phillip Chancellor IV	1993
Vivica A. Fox	Stephanie Simmons	1995
Cam Gigandet	Daniel Romalotti	Temporary; 2004
David Hasselhoff	Snapper Foster (#2)	1975–1982, 2010
Alex D. Linz	Phillip Chancellor IV	1995

Eva Longoria	Isabella Braña Williams	2001–2003
Shemar Moore	Malcolm Winters	1994–2002, 2004–2005
Monica Potter	Sharon Abbott	Temporary; 1994
Tom Selleck	Jed Andrews	1974–1975
Paul Walker	Brandon Collins	1992–1993

Notable celebrities who have had regular roles

Actor	Character	Duration	Source
Robert Colbert	Stuart Brooks	1973–1983	
Clementine Ford	Mackenzie Browning (#4)	2009–	
Michael Gross	River Baldwin	2008–2009	
Nia Peeples	Karen Winters	2007–2009	
Francesco Quinn	Tomas Del Cerro	1999–2001	
Tammin Sursok	Colleen Carlton (#3)	2007–2009	
Joan Van Ark	Gloria Bardwell (#1)	2004–2005	

Notable celebrity cameos

- Composer Andrew Lloyd Webber appeared on a 1993 episode to personally invite Michael Damian's character Danny Romalotti to play the lead in a revival production of Webber's "Joseph and the Amazing Technicolor Dreamcoat." This set up Damian's hiatus from *The Young and the Restless* to play the title role in a Los Angeles production of Joseph.
- A1, a British boy band, appeared at the prom in 2002.
- Chris Botti played at Michael and Lauren's wedding 2005.
- Wayne Brady and his 'real life' mother visited with Paul and Mary Williams on Mother's Day 2003.
- Peter Cincotti appeared in 2003 to surprise Christine.
- Robert Clary (of *Hogan's Heroes* fame) was part of the series original regular cast members when the show premiered.
- Colby Donaldson (of *Survivor: The Australian Outback*) flirted in 2004 with Brittany before noticing her scar at the opening of the Rec Center.
- Josh Gracin, former *American Idol* contestant, appeared as a cowboy in June 2006.
- Wayne Gretzky appeared as Wayne on November 12, 1981.
- Enrique Iglesias, Latino singer, will appear as himself in November 2007.

- Il Divo appeared in 2005 to surprise Nikki.
- Jewel appeared on May 31, 2006 to sing at a benefit in memory of Cassie Newman.
- Brian Jordan of the *Atlanta Braves* appeared as himself on the show on 2 or 3 different occasions.
- George Kennedy appeared as Victor's father in 2003.
- B. B. King appeared in 2001.
- Darlene Koldenhoven appeared and sang while Nikki walked down the aisle in 2002.
- Kenny Lattimore and Chanté Moore appeared in December 2003 as special guests at Neil and Dru's wedding.
- Reichen Lehmkuhl of *The Amazing Race* has played Katherine Chancellor's bartender.
- Tara Lipinski, Olympic Gold medalist, playing Megan Dennison's friend Marnie Kowalski in 1999.
- Rich Little; appeared in the 1980s when Brad's ex-wife, Lisa, had him mimic Brad's voice on a tape.
- Michael McDonald; appeared in the 1980s, performing "Sweet Freedom" during Danny Romalotti's concert.
- Jerri Manthey of *Survivor: The Australian Outback* discussed a Jabot promotional contract with Jill.
- Lionel Richie appeared in 2001 at a club visited by Sean Bridges and Jill.
- Smokey Robinson appeared in 2004 to give J.T. advice about the music business.
- Jesse Ventura appeared as himself in 2001.
- Luke Walton appeared as himself in 2006, played a pick-up game of basketball with Neil Winters.
- Lee Philip Bell appeared as herself on the September 11, 2006 episode.
- Will Kirby of Big Brother appeared on the October 23, 2006 episode, talking to Jack at Jabot.
- Aaron Neville appeared as himself, singing at the opening of Neil and Dru's jazz club "Indigo" on October 27, 2006.
- Sylvia Browne appeared as herself for several episodes.
- Glenda Hatchett appeared as a judge on the episode seen on December 14, 2006.
- J. J. Hardy, Bill Hall, Jeff Suppan and Chris Capuano of The Milwaukee Brewers Baseball Club appeared on June 20, 2007.
- Enrique Iglesias appeared as himself, singing at *Indigo* on November 7, 2007.
- Pat Benatar and Neil Giraldo appeared as themselves on February 14 and 15, 2008 at Indigo.
- Trace Adkins appeared as himself, singing at the Restless Style office for Phyllis' and Nick's anniversary on May 2, 2008.
- Kathy Hilton appeared as herself at the Restless Style office on May 13, 2008.
- Katy Perry appeared as herself for the cover of Restless Style Magazine on Thursday, June 12, 2008.

Crossovers

The Young and the Restless and *The Bold and the Beautiful*

There have been several crossovers between *The Young and the Restless* and sister show *The Bold and the Beautiful*:

- **1992**

  - ***The Bold and the Beautiful*:** Sheila Carter (Kimberlin Brown) was the first major character to cross over to *The Bold and the Beautiful*. Sheila appeared on *The Young and the Restless* from 1990-1992 (returning as a guest in 1993, 1994 and 1995), and again in 2005-2006. She was on *The Bold and the Beautiful* from 1992–1998, with shorter-lived stints in 2002 and 2003.

  - ***The Bold and the Beautiful*:** Molly Carter (Marilyn Alex) appeared several times after her daughter, Sheila, was revealed to be living in Los Angeles.

- **1993**

  - ***The Young and the Restless*:** Eric Forrester (John McCook) called Lauren from his office to invite her to Los Angeles.

  - ***The Bold and the Beautiful*:** Brad Carlton (Don Diamont) crossed over to confront Sheila Carter about the photos of his tryst with Lauren Fenmore (Tracey E. Bregman), fearing that he would lose custody of his daughter, Colleen, if they became public. Although Brad's threats were enough to make Sheila give up the photos, Lauren later discovered that there was still more evidence proving their affair.

  - ***The Young and the Restless*:** Stephanie Forrester (Susan Flannery) appeared on *The Young and the Restless* to inform Lauren of Sheila's marriage to Eric.

  - ***The Bold and the Beautiful*:** Dr. Scott Grainger (Peter Barton) and Lauren Fenmore were vacationing on Catalina Island where they were shocked to find Eric Forrester and Sheila Carter also on a romantic retreat. The character Scott Grainger died during this crossover, but not before he forgave Sheila for her past and begged Lauren not to reveal their history to Eric.

- **1995**

  - ***The Young and the Restless*:** Eric Forrester (John McCook) appears at his office in Los Angeles to inform Sheila that Lauren will be coming to town.

  - ***The Young and the Restless*:** James Warwick (Ian Buchanan) made a brief crossover when he called Lauren from Sheila's dungeon. Brad Carlton also makes an appearance.

  - ***The Bold and the Beautiful*:** Lauren Fenmore (Tracey E. Bregman) crossed over to *The Bold and the Beautiful*, where she stayed until 1999, and briefly returned in 2002 and 2004. She had already appeared on the show several times prior to her becoming an actual cast member, mostly due to Sheila's crossover in 1992.

- **1998**

- *The Young and the Restless*: Brooke Logan (Katherine Kelly Lang) crossed over to meet with Victor Newman (Eric Braeden) at his Newman Enterprises office in Genoa City, Wisconsin. In her effort to spice up the deal she's trying to work out, Brooke drops her jacket and reveals that she is wearing very little. Much to Victor's chagrin (and possible enjoyment), Brad Carlton (Don Diamont) and Jack Abbott (Peter Bergman) walk in on the scene.
- *The Bold and the Beautiful*: Jack Abbott (Peter Bergman) crossed over to meet with Eric Forrester (John McCook), Brooke Logan (Katherine Kelly Lang), Ridge Forrester (Ronn Moss), and Thorne Forrester (Winsor Harmon). The Forresters were looking for a new scent to go along with Brooke's Bedroom Line, and thought that Jabot Cosmetics could help.

- **1999**

  - *The Bold and the Beautiful*: Victor Newman (Eric Braeden) appeared to meet with Brooke Logan (Katherine Kelly Lang)...and to make Ridge Forrester (Ronn Moss) jealous. With prodding from Brooke, Victor agreed to kiss her, thus enraging Ridge and ruining his night out with Dr. Taylor Hayes Forrester (Hunter Tylo).

- **2000-2001**

  - *The Bold and the Beautiful*: Dr. Tim Reid (Aaron Lustig), who was Phyllis Summers' therapist, moved to Los Angeles and helped Morgan DeWitt (Sarah Buxton).

- **2003**

  - *The Bold and the Beautiful*: Lauren Fenmore's (Tracey E. Bregman) mother, Joanna Manning (Susan Seaforth Hayes), appeared in her capacity as a ranking employee of Fenmore's Department Stores.

- **2004**

  - *The Bold and the Beautiful*: Lauren Fenmore (Tracey E. Bregman) received an angered phone call from the husband of her employee Jacqueline Payne Marone, who demanded to know if the two had really gone out drinking the night before like he was being told. Although she was caught off-guard, Lauren said they had, assuming Jacquie had a good reason for lying to her husband. In truth, Jacquie had told her husband this to help cover up her one night stand with Deacon Sharpe Sean Kanan.

- **2005**

  - *The Young and the Restless*: Eric Forrester (John McCook) crossed over twice: Once to warn Michael Baldwin (Christian LeBlanc) about Sheila Carter, and a second time to attend the wedding of Michael and Lauren Fenmore.
  - *The Bold and the Beautiful*: While eating lunch at a restaurant in Los Angeles, Katherine Chancellor (Jeanne Cooper) was approached by Massimo Marone (Joseph Mascolo). Massimo introduced her to friend Stephanie Douglas Forrester (Susan Flannery), the daughter of an old business acquaintance Katherine used to know (John Douglas). It was learned that Katherine was

the actual owner of Forrester Creations, which Stephanie sought to reclaim from her estranged husband Eric Forrester. With Katherine's blessing, Stephanie achieved her goal, leaving the grand dame of Genoa City free to focus on her numerous other assets.

- Lauren's mother, Joanna Manning (Susan Seaforth Hayes), appeared on both *The Bold and the Beautiful* and *The Young and the Restless* (the latter in December to attend her daughter's wedding to Michael Baldwin).

- **2006**

  - *The Young and the Restless*: In November, Amber Moore (Adrienne Frantz) arrived in Genoa City to stay.

- **2007**

  - *The Bold and the Beautiful*: Lauren Fenmore appeared in January.
  - *The Bold and the Beautiful*: Ashley Abbott (Eileen Davidson) crossed over in early March when Eric Forrester put plans in motion to launch a fragrance line for his new fashion house, Forrester Originals.
  - *The Bold and the Beautiful*: Traci (Beth Maitland), Ashley Abbott's sister, also appeared in March, while talking to her sister on the telephone.
  - *The Bold and the Beautiful*: Abby Carlton (Darcy Rose Byrnes) joined Ashley in Los Angeles in May.
  - *The Bold and the Beautiful*: Christine Blair (Lauralee Bell) arrived in Los Angeles in June to defend Ridge Forrester (Ronn Moss) after he was arrested for the murder of Shane McGrath (Dax Griffin). Christine got the charges dropped after Rick Forrester's (Kyle Lowder) testimony. The Forresters thanked Christine and she returned to Genoa City.
  - *The Young and the Restless*: Brooke Logan (Katherine Kelly Lang), while at her office in Los Angeles, received a phone call from Cane Ashby (Daniel Goddard) regarding his wife, Amber Moore. Brooke filled Cane in on her history with Amber, leaivng Cane with even more questions about his marriage.

- **2008**

  - *The Young and the Restless*: Ashley Abbott (Eileen Davidson) returned to visit her brother Jack Abbott and Victor Newman in January.
  - *The Young and the Restless*: Eric Forrester (John McCook) met with Jack Abbott in February about the magazine *Restless Style* at Forrester Creations. During that same trip to Los Angeles, Jack and his wife, Sharon Abbott (Sharon Case), paid a visit to Ashley Abbott (Eileen Davidson).
  - *The Young and the Restless*: In March, Ashley Abbott (Eileen Davidson) and Felicia Forrester (Lesli Kay) flew to Genoa City for the launch of the magazine *Restless Syle*.
  - *The Young and the Restless*: Felicia Forrester (Lesli Kay) crossed over in April on recurring status.

- *The Young and the Restless*: Ashley Abbott (Eileen Davidson) crossed over to go head-to-head with her former stepmother Gloria Bardwell (Judith Chapman) in June.
- *The Young and the Restless*: Ashley Abbott (Eileen Davidson) returned to *The Young and the Restless* permanently in September 2008.

- **2009**
  - *The Young and the Restless*: Sean Kanan signed a contract to reprise his *Bold and the Beautiful* role as Deacon Sharpe on *The Young and the Restless*.

- **2010**
  - **The Young and the Restless**: Amber's Mother, Tawny Moore (Andrea Evans), appeared on the May 12 episode looking for Amber after she left town with little Eric.
  - **The Bold and the Beautiful**: Amber Moore (Adrienne Frantz), back on *The Bold and the Beautiful* after four years.

- **Possible Connection**
  - The actor Robert Clary played Pierre Roulland on *The Young and the Restless* from 1973-1974 before playing Pierre Jourdan on *The Bold and the Beautiful* from 1990-1992. Whether or not the two characters are related is unknown.

The Young and the Restless and *As the World Turns*

There have been three notable crossovers between *The Young and the Restless* and *As the World Turns*:

- **2005**
  - *As the World Turns*: Michael Baldwin (Christian LeBlanc) traveled to Oakdale to argue part of a custody case involving Jack Snyder (Michael Park) and Julia Larrabee.

- **2007**
  - *The Young and the Restless*: The character of Alison Stewart met with Amber Moore on February 22, 2007. (Note: Alison was played by a different actress than before on *As the World Turns*. The "new" Alison then returned to Oakdale in March.
  - *The Young and the Restless*: Emily Stewart (Kelley Menighan Hensley) sought-out Amber Moore at Crimson Lights Coffeehouse, in Genoa City, in March 2007. She wanted to know the whereabouts of her sister Alison, but Amber pretended not to know. Once Emily was gone, Amber called Alison to give her a heads-up.

Other shows/films

- *The Young and the Restless* cast members Melody Thomas Scott, Peter Bergman, Joshua Morrow and Shemar Moore, along with *The Bold and the Beautiful*'s Hunter Tylo and Barbara Crampton, appeared as themselves on the CBS sitcom *The Nanny* (1997)
- In an episode of the sitcom *The King of Queens*, several *The Young and the Restless* cast members appeared in Doug Heffernan's (Kevin James) dream.

- In the 1990s, many actors from *The Young and the Restless* appeared on the CBS drama *Diagnosis: Murder* (including Eric Braeden, Melody Thomas Scott, Heather Tom, Kristoff St. John, Lauralee Bell, Doug Davidson, J. Eddie Peck, and Kimberlin Brown) in which Victoria Rowell's character on *Diagnosis: Murder*, Dr. Amanda Bently, won a walk-on appearance on *The Young and the Restless*.

References

- http://www.soaps.com/youngandrestless/comings_and_goings/

Biographies of Senior Cast Members

Jeanne Cooper

Jeanne Cooper	
Born	Wilma Jeanne Cooper October 25, 1928 Taft, California, U.S.
Occupation	Actress
Years active	1953–present
Spouse	Harry Bernsen (1954-1977)

Wilma Jeanne Cooper (born October 25, 1928 in Taft, California), best known as **Jeanne Cooper**, is an American actress best known for her portrayal of Katherine Chancellor on the daytime soap opera *The Young and the Restless*. Though she was not on the series when the show debuted in March 1973, she made her onscreen debut in November of that year, and remains the longest-tenured actor on *The Young and the Restless*.

Early career

Cooper began her career in the 1950s. Her first starring role was as Myra in 1953's western *The Redhead from Wyoming*. She also appeared as a player in films with stars like Maureen O'Hara, Glenn Ford, Tony Curtis, and Henry Fonda. Cooper was a fixture on episodic television throughout the 1960s and 1970s.

In 1965, she appeared in the western "The Big Valley" as Heath's money hungry aunt. Her husband was portrayed by John Anderson, who years later became known as MacGyver's often quoted grandfather, Harry Jackson.

Katherine Chancellor (Katherine Reynolds, Chancellor, Thurston, Sterling, Murphy (née Shepherd))

Cooper's character has broken ground in the daytime medium; Katherine has endured several bouts with alcoholism, and the loss of many men in her life (four late husbands, and a child given away after birth).

Katherine (and Cooper) also had a facelift on national television (Cooper had pitched the idea of having a live facelift to CBS executives, who agreed to write the facelift into the show for Katherine Chancellor).

For many years, the story of Katherine's bitter rivalry with character Jill Foster Abbott has been a mainstay of the show. (In real life, Cooper and Jill's portrayer, Jess Walton are close friends.) It was revealed in 2003 that Jill was Katherine's daughter born out of wedlock, but developments in 2009 have cast doubt upon that assertion and the long bitter enemies were found not to be Mother and Daughter after all.

She has received nine Daytime Emmy nominations, eight for Outstanding Lead Actress and one for Outstanding Supporting Actress, and two Primetime Emmy nominations. She received a Lifetime Achievement Award from the Daytime Emmys in 2004. For her contributions to television, Cooper received a star on the Hollywood Walk of Fame, which is located at 6801 Hollywood Blvd. She won the 2008 Daytime Emmy Award for Outstanding Lead Actress in a Drama Series. Out of her eight nominations for lead actress, this was her first win in the category.

Cooper also played the role of Marge Cotrooke, Katherine's lookalike, on the show from 1989 to 1990, and again in 2008 and 2009. Cooper recently signed a new three-year deal with *Y&R*.

Cooper's character, Katherine, was thought to have died in a November 2008 episode. It was, however, her look-alike Marge who died, and Katherine is currently experiencing memory issues due to the car accident that took Marge's life.

Cooper's character, Katherine, along with Christian LeBlanc's character, Michael, made a guest appearance on the finale of *Guiding Light* which aired Friday, September 18, 2009.

Personal life

Jeanne Cooper was born to Albert Troy Cooper and his wife Sildeth Evelyn Moore. She was the youngest of their three children. Jeanne's family lived in Kern County for several years, first in Taft until 1942 and then moving to Bakersfield. Her mother died August 21, 1945 and her father died April 11, 1986. She married television producer Harry Bernsen, Jr. and they were together 23 years before divorcing. Interviews and reports state they remained the best of friends until his death in June 2008.

The Bernsens had three children, including actor Corbin Bernsen, of *L.A. Law* fame (Ms. Cooper guest-starred twice as his character's mother on the series) born September 7, 1954 who is married to British actress Amanda Pays. Another son who is an actor, Collin Bernsen, born March 30, 1958. She also has a daughter, Caren. born August 17, 1960 who is an actress.

Corbin Bernsen and Amanda Pays have four sons: Oliver Miller (born 1989), twins Henry and Angus (born 1992), and Finley (born 1998)

Selected filmography

Show	Character	Duration
The Young and the Restless	Katherine Chancellor Marge Cotrooke	1973–Present 1989-1990, 2008, 2009
The Bold and the Beautiful	Katherine Chancellor	2005 (guest in two episodes)
Donna On Demand	Virginia Hart	2009
Guiding Light	Wedding Guest	2009 (guest star)
Carpool Guy	Mrs. Lunsford	2004
Sweet Hostage	Mrs. Withers	1975
Kansas City Bomber	Trainer Vivien	1972
The Intruder (1962 film)	Vi Griffin	1962
Perry Mason	Laura Beaumont Thelma Hill Ethel Belan Mary Browne Miriam Fielding	1958 1959 1962 1964 1966
Shadows of Tombstone	Marge	1953
The Redhead from Wyoming	Myra	1953

External links

- Jeanne Cooper [1] at the Internet Movie Database
- Jeanne Cooper [2] at TV.com
- Jeanne Cooper bio [3] on *The Young and the Restless* CBS website

Doug Davidson

Doug Davidson	
Born	Douglas Donald Davidson October 24, 1954 Glendale, California, U.S.
Occupation	Actor
Years active	1978—present

Douglas Donald "Doug" Davidson (born October 24, 1954 in Glendale, California) is an American television actor. He has portrayed private investigator Paul Williams on the CBS soap opera *The Young and the Restless* since May 1978, making him the series' senior male cast member.

On September 12, 1994, he began hosting a five-night-a-week, syndicated, half hour version of the game show *The New Price Is Right*, but the show was canceled just four and a half months later on January 27, 1995 due to both the O. J. Simpson trial and a product that was generally seen as too much of a departure from the familiar daytime version. Davidson was one of a few people given an audition to replace Bob Barker after his retirement from *The Price Is Right* in 2007, a role which ultimately went to Drew Carey. Davidson has also hosted the live stage show adaptation, *The Price Is Right Live!*, at Harrah's-owned casinos in Las Vegas, Nevada.

From 1998 through 2003, Davidson served as a host of the annual Tournament of Roses Parade. Davidson was seen as the leader of the *The Young and the Restless* team when they played for charity on the CBS and syndicated Ray Combs era of *Family Feud* in the early 1990s.

He has been married to actress Cindy Fisher since 1984. They have two children, daughter Calyssa and son Caden.

Roles

- *The Young and the Restless* – Paul Williams (May 1978–present)
- *L.A. Johns* (1997)
- *Mr. Write* – Roger (1994)
- *The New Price Is Right* (1994–1995)
- *I'll Take Manhattan* (1987)
- *The Initiation of Sarah* – Tommy (1978)

Awards and nominations

- Daytime Emmy Award nomination, Outstanding Lead Actor (2010)
- Daytime Emmy Award nomination, Outstanding Lead Actor (2003)
- Daytime Emmy Award pre-nomination, Outstanding Lead Actor (2003, 2004)
- Soap Opera Digest Awards – Winner, Best Supporting Actor (1992, 1997)
- Soap Opera Digest Awards – Winner, Outstanding Hero (1990, 1991)

External links

- Doug Davidson [1] at the Internet Movie Database

Melody Thomas Scott

Melody Thomas Scott	
Melody Thomas Scott in 2007 Photo credit to JPI Studios	
Born	Melody Ann Thomas April 18, 1956 Los Angeles, California, U.S.
Occupation	Actress
Years active	1964 – present
Spouse	Edward J. Scott

Melody Thomas Scott (born April 18, 1956) is an American actress best known for playing Nikki Newman on the soap opera *The Young and the Restless*.

Early life & acting career

Scott was born **Melody Ann Thomas** in Los Angeles, California. Her first film credit was as a child actress in the 1964 Alfred Hitchcock movie *Marnie*. After bit parts in movies in the mid-'70s (most notably in John Wayne's final film, *The Shootist* in 1976), she was offered bit parts on nighttime series such as *The Waltons*, *The Rockford Files*, and *Charlie's Angels*.

In 1979, at the age of 23, she began playing the part of stripper Nikki Reed on the daytime serial *The Young and the Restless*, choosing the part over a sitcom pilot that in the end was not picked up. She was a replacement for the previous Nikki, who had lasted six months. Over time, her character reformed and became an important part of Genoa City society, as she married Victor Newman (Eric Braeden). Scott has said, "It's a miracle for an actor to have a job last 28 years," although she finds it frustrating to go through periods when she doesn't have a storyline.

Scott was parodied in the satire publication *The Onion* in 1999, in which a picture was edited to show her holding a Daytime Emmy (that year, Susan Lucci won the Emmy after 19 nominations). The caption read "Awards Given Out Randomly To Skinny Blonde Women". She appeared on various game shows over the years, including *Family Feud* (with various *Young and the Restless* co-stars), *Pyramid*, *Body Language*, and *Match Game*.

Personal life

She has been married to the supervising producer of *Y&R*, Edward J. Scott, since October 1985. The couple, who have three daughters, Elizabeth, Alexandra, and Jennifer, renewed their vows in an elaborate ceremony that doubled as their 20th wedding anniversary in June 2005. Melody got divorced from husband Edward May 25, 2010, ending a blistful marriage and Edward cut all ties with Young and the Restless.

Scott was one of the original board members of the Lucille Ball-Desi Arnaz Center in Jamestown, New York. She resigned in protest of the Center's behavior under its Executive Director Ric Wyman, on July 17, 2008.

Filmography

- *Marnie* - Young Marnie (1964)
- *Dirty Harry* - Ann Mary Deacon [photographs] (uncredited) (1971)
- *The Beguiled* - Abigail (1971)
- *Posse* - Laurie (1975)
- *The Shootist* - Girl on streetcar (1976)
- *The Car* - Suzie (1977)
- *The Fury* - LaRue (1978)
- *Piranha* - Laura Dickinson (1978)
- *The Young And The Restless* - Nikki Newman (February 1979 - present)
- *The Paradise Virus* - Linda Flemming (2003), written by Peter Layton, co-starring Lorenzo Lamas, and directed and produced by Brian Trenchard-Smith

Awards and nominations

- Daytime Emmys Nomination, Outstanding Lead Actress (1999)
- Daytime Emmys Pre-Nomination, Outstanding Lead Actress (2005, 2008)

See also

- Victor Newman and Nikki Reed
- Supercouple

External links

- Melody Thomas Scott [1] at the Internet Movie Database
- Melody's official page [2]

Eric Braeden

<table>
<tr><td colspan="2" align="center">**Eric Braeden**</td></tr>
<tr><td colspan="2" align="center">
Eric Braeden in 2007</td></tr>
<tr><td>**Born**</td><td>Hans Jörg Gudegast
April 3, 1941
Bredenbek, Germany</td></tr>
<tr><td>**Occupation**</td><td>Actor</td></tr>
<tr><td>**Years active**</td><td>1960–present</td></tr>
<tr><td>**Spouse**</td><td>Dale Russell Gudegast (1966-present); 1 child</td></tr>
<tr><td colspan="2" align="center">**Website**</td></tr>
<tr><td colspan="2" align="center">http://www.ericbraeden.com</td></tr>
</table>

Eric Braeden (born **Hans Jörg Gudegast** on April 3, 1941) is a German-born film and television actor, best known for his role as Victor Newman on the soap opera *The Young and the Restless*. Braeden won a Daytime Emmy Award in 1998 for Lead Actor in a Drama Series for the role.

Early life

Braeden was born **Hans Jörg Gudegast** in Bredenbek, Germany (near Kiel), where his father was once mayor. He emigrated to the USA in 1959. In the United States, Braeden attended The University of Montana in Missoula.

Career

Braeden accumulated many TV and film credits during his first two decades in America, most notably a role as the German Hauptmann (Captain) Hans Dietrich on the TV series *The Rat Patrol* (1966–1968), as well as a starring role in the movie *Colossus: The Forbin Project* (1970), in which he first took the stage name of Eric Braeden, and a supporting role in the 1971 film *Escape from the Planet of the Apes*. He was also kept busy during the early 1970s in a variety of guest starring roles in such TV series as *The Mary Tyler Moore Show* and *Wonder Woman* and as a guest star in several episodes of the CBS western *Gunsmoke*. He also appeared, uncredited, as Bradford Dillman's *de facto* stunt double in the 1978 film *Piranha*--Braeden had originally been cast to play Dillman's character, Paul Grogan, and had shot some underwater swimming footage before the role was recast; Braeden's stunt footage ended up in the finished film anyway.

In 1980, he was offered the role of self-made magnate Victor Newman on *The Young and the Restless* for a 26-week run. His character imprisoned his wife's lover, and became so popular the character became a love-to-hate villain, and his contract was renewed. Still on the show today, Braeden won a Daytime Emmy for his work in 1998.

In late December 1991, Braeden and Peter Bergman had a physical altercation backstage. According to press reports,[*citation needed*] after exchanging bitter words on the set, Braeden showed up at Bergman's dressing room door to further discuss the matter and violence ensued. Y&R's creator and senior executive producer William J. Bell threaten to fire them both if it ever happened again. Since then, the actors have resolved their differences and now enjoy a cordial relationship.

In 1997, he played Colonel John Jacob Astor IV in the blockbuster film *Titanic*, picked because he strongly resembled the powerful millionaire.

In 2008, Braeden starred in "The Man Who Came Back," an independent Western film of double-cross and revenge, which was written and directed by Louisiana's Glen Pitre.

Braeden starred in a *How I Met Your Mother* episode (November 3, 2008) as Robin Sr., Robin's father, trying to make his daughter act like the son he never had. He then has an emotional breakdown when he realizes that he "has no son".

Braeden announced on October 18, 2009, in an article by Dan J. Kroll that after almost 30 years on *The Young and the Restless*, he was leaving the show. "We reached an impasse in the negotiations", Braeden said in an exclusive interview with celebrity news website EW.com. Braeden's last airdate was scheduled to be November 2; however, on October 23, 2009, CBS announced that Braeden had inked a new three-year deal and would remain with the soap, even agreeing to take a pay cut, which was the original issue.

Personal life

Braeden is regarded as a very good tennis player. He and his wife, Dale Gudegast, were witnesses at the wedding of Bob Crane and Sigrid Valdis while on the set of *Hogan's Heroes*. Their son, Christian Gudegast, is a screenwriter who co-wrote the film *A Man Apart*, which starred Vin Diesel and was nominated for a *Teen Choice Award* in 2003.

Actor Clarence Williams III and former boxer Ken Norton are two of his best friends.

Awards, honors and nominations

Braeden won a Daytime Emmy Award in 1998 for Lead Actor in a Drama Series for his work on *The Young and the Restless*.

On July 20, 2007, he received a star on the Hollywood Walk of Fame.

Braeden received the Gilmore Award from the Pacific Pioneers, a radio and television industry group, in 2007.

* Daytime Emmys -Winner, Outstanding Lead Actor in a Drama Series (1998)
* Daytime Emmys Nomination, Outstanding Lead Actor in a Drama Series (1987, 1990, 1996, 1997, 1998, 1999, 2000, 2004)
* Daytime Emmys Pre-Nomination, Outstanding Lead Actor in a Drama Series (2004, 2005, 2008)
* 18th Annual People's Choice Award for Most Popular Daytime Actor
* Distinguished German-American of the Year 1990

He received the 2009 Friend of German Award from the American Association of Teachers of German.

Roles

Year	Title	Role
1963	*Combat!*	Hans Gruber
1963–1964	*The Hostages*	
1965?	*Combat!*	Ecktmann
1966–1967	*Mission: Impossible*	Andrei Fetyakov
1966–1968	*The Rat Patrol*	Hauptmann (Captain) Hans Dietrich
1969	*Hawaii Five-O*	Dr. Paul Farrar

1970	*Hawaii Five-O*	Klaus Marburg
	Colossus: The Forbin Project	Dr. Charles A. Forbin
	The Mask of Sheba	Dr. Morgan
1971	*Escape from the Planet of the Apes*	Dr. Otto Hasslein
1971	*Bearcats!*	Col. Reinert
1972	*The Judge and Jake Wyler*	Anton Granicek
1973	*The Adulteress*	Hank Baron
	The Six Million Dollar Man	Findletter
1974	*Kolchak: The Night Stalker*	Bernhardt Stieglitz
	Banacek	Paul Bolitho
	The Ultimate Thrill	Roland
1975	*Wonder Woman*	Evan Donaldson
1977	*Kojak*	Kenneth Krug
	Herbie Goes to Monte Carlo	Bruno von Stickle
1979	*CHiPs*	Senator Lerwin
1980	*The Young and the Restless*	Victor Newman
1981	*Charlie's Angels*	John Reardon
1990	*Lucky/Chances*	Dimitri Stanislopolous
1994	*The Nanny*	Frank Bradley, Sr.
1995	*Diagnosis: Murder*	Himself
1997	*Titanic*	John Jacob Astor IV
1998	*Meet the Deedles*	Elton Deedle
1999	*The Bold and the Beautiful*	Victor Newman
2008	*The Man Who Came Back*	Reese Paxton
	How I Met Your Mother	Robin Scherbatsky, Sr.

ed - The Eric Braeden Project: A Conversation with Eric Braeden [5] 2010 interview with Eric Braeden
- Interview on The Gregory Mantell Show [6]
- Distinguished German-American of the Year 1990 by the German-American Heritage Foundation of the USA in Washington, DC [7]
- Tonight Eric Braeden Will Eat Your Soul: A Look At the Pre-Soap Career of TV's Black Knight [8] at Confessions of a Pop Culture Addict

Eileen Davidson

Eileen Davidson	
Born	June 15, 1959 Artesia, California
Spouse	Vincent Van Patten (15 April 2003 - present) 1 child Jon Lindstrom (3 May 1997 - 2000) (divorced) Christopher Mayer (1985 - 1986) (divorced)

Eileen Davidson (born June 15, 1959) is an American film and soap opera actress. She is known for her role as Ashley Abbott on *The Young and the Restless* and *The Bold and the Beautiful* and for the multiple roles she portrayed on *Days of our Lives*.

Biography

Personal life

Davidson was born in Artesia, California, daughter of Charlotte, a homemaker, and Richard Davidson, an airplane parts manufacturer.

Davidson has been married three times: first to actor Christopher Mayer from 1985-1986. Her second husband was former *General Hospital* and *Port Charles* and current *As the World Turns* actor Jon Lindstrom, to whom she was married from 1997 to 2000. She is currently married to actor Vince Van Patten. They have 1 chid together: Jesse (born in 2003). They met when he briefly appeared as her "boyfriend" on a cruise.

Davidson is related to several well-known actors, actresses, singers and an athlete through her marriage to Vince. Vince's father is actor Dick Van Patten ("Eight is Enough"). Dick's sister is actress Joyce Van Patten. Joyce was married to actor Martin Balsam. Joyce and Martin's daughter is actress Talia Balsam ("Mad Men"). Talia's first husband was actor George Clooney. George's father is famed journalist and host Nick Clooney. Nick's sister was singer Rosemary Clooney. Rosemary was married to actor Jose Ferrer. Jose Ferrer was a cousin of tennis pro Gigi Fernandez. One of Rosemary and Jose's sons is actor Miguel Ferrer ("Crossing Jordan," "Traffic"). Miguel's brother, Gabriel Ferrer, is married to singer Debby Boone. Debby's father is singer Pat Boone. Talia Balsam's second husband is actor John Slattery ("Mad Men," "Sex and the City," "Desperate Housewives").

Career

Davidson started her career as a model in Mexico City and California, eventually adding commercials and print work in Europe. Her agent had recommended that she take acting classes to get work in commercials, but she took to acting so well that she was sent out to auditions for acting roles. She originated the role of Ashley Abbott on *The Young and the Restless* in March 1982, beating out more than 100 candidates. The character of Ashley became a front-burner character, and Davidson became an integral part of the show. She quit the show in December 1988 and the producers took her recommendation of hiring a look-alike actress named Brenda Epperson Doumani, whom Davidson had discovered waiting tables at a charity function.

Davidson then appeared in primetime television, but her show, *Broken Badges* (1990-1991), was canceled. She returned to daytime when she assumed the role of Kelly Capwell on *Santa Barbara* from May 1991 until the soap's cancellation in January 1993. She next appeared as Kristen Blake on *Days of our Lives* beginning in May 1993. As originally conceived, Kristen was a heroine, who had an Achilles' heel in that the show's supervillain, Stefano, had raised her after the death of her parents. James E. Reilly, who assumed head writing reins in 1993, began to make Kristen more of a villainess. Reilly eventually developed an outrageous second role for Davidson, having her play Susan Banks, a Kristen look-alike. Reilly eventually penned three more roles for Davidson (Sister Mary Moira, Thomas, and Penelope). Davidson enjoyed the challenge, but after playing so many multiple characters and making daytime television history, she decided to take a breather and leave the show. Her character, Kristen, intended to keep her other character, Susan, prisoner on an island, but Susan ultimately prevailed and Kristen has remained on the island and has not been heard from since. All related characters were last seen in May 1998. Davidson's five roles earned her a Daytime Emmy nomination for Outstanding Lead Actress in 1998.

After a year-long vacation, she returned to her role on *The Young and the Restless* in March 1999. After a successful return as Ashley Abbott, which included Davidson's second Daytime Emmy nomination for Outstanding Lead Actress, Davidson was fired from the show. In December 2006, Davidson told *TV Guide* that she was fired from *The Young and the Restless* due to lack of storyline. Her last airdate as Ashley was January 11, 2007. According to co-star Melody Thomas Scott, the firing was protested behind the scenes of *The Young and the Restless* and was seen as unfair. Scott said: "That was so heartbreaking. We're still upset about that. That was a blow. Terrible. Eileen Davidson was such a part of the core of the show and such a brilliant actress; beautiful and always prepared. It was crazy. I'm not the only one who feels that way."

In a surprise move a few months later, Davidson signed a three-year contract with *The Young and the Restless*'s sister soap *The Bold and the Beautiful* to once again play her *The Young and the Restless* character Ashley Abbott at the request of *The Bold and the Beautiful* executive producer Bradley Bell. She first aired on March 9, 2007.

Ken Corday called Davidson about a week before she was fired from *The Young and the Restless* to get permission to use a picture of her on *Days of our Lives*. The picture, which featured Davidson as Susan, was shown in December 2006.

After she was fired from *The Young and the Restless* but before being cast in *The Bold and the Beautiful*, her niece Devon Martt, a fashion designer, approached her about designing clothes together. Davidson liked the idea and formed a clothing company called Femmeology.

Davidson co-wrote her first novel with author Robert J. Randisi, a mystery set in the soap opera world titled *Death in Daytime*, released in October 2008. Her second mystery novel, *Dial Emmy for Murder,* was released in June 2009. She is working on her third mystery novel, *Diva Las Vegas*.

In July 2008, Eileen was downgraded to recurring status at *The Bold and the Beautiful*. She returned to *The Young and the Restless* full-time as Ashley on September 26, 2008.

Filmography

- 1982: *The Phoenix* as Ellie (1 episode)
- 1982 - present: *The Young and the Restless* as Ashley Abbott (1982-1988, March 19, 1999-January 11, 2007, December 28, 2007-January 3, 2008; February 27 and 28, 2008; March 25 and 26, 2008; June 19, 20 and 23, 2008, September 26, 2008 - present)
- 1982: *Goin' All the Way* as BJ
- 1983: *The House on Sorority Row* as Vicki
- 1988: *Sharing Richard* as J.C. Dennison
- 1989: *Eternity* as Dahlia/Valerie
- 1989: *Easy Wheels* as She Wolf
- 1990: *Broken Badges* as J.J. 'Bullet' Tingreedes (3 episodes)
- 1992 - 1993: *Santa Barbara* as Kelly Capwell (24 episodes)
- 1993 - 1998: *Days of our Lives* as Penelope Kent (1998), Thomas Banks (1997), Sister Mary Moira Banks (1997 - 1998), Susan Banks (November 4, 1996 - April 8,1998), Kristen Blake DiMera (1993 - 1998)
- 2007 - 2008: *The Bold and the Beautiful* as Ashley Abbott (March 9, 2007-July 4, 2008; November 25, 2008)
- 2010: *Symphoria*

Awards and nominations

1. Emmy nomination as Outstanding Lead Actress in a daytime Serial--Days of our Lives (1998)
2. Emmy nomination as Outstanding Lead Actress in a daytime Serial--The Young and the Restless (2003).

External links

- Eileen's Official Website [1]
- Eileen's Official Facebook Page [2]
- Eileen Davidson Online (Fansite) [3]
- Eileen Davidson [4] at the Internet Movie Database
- Ashley Abbott Carlton character profile on SoapCentral [5]
- CBS-TV: *The Young and the Restless* [3]

Kate Linder

Kate Linder	
 Linder at a fashion show in January 2008	
Born	November 2, 1947 Pasadena, California, USA

Kate Linder (born November 2, 1947) is an American actress, best known for her role as Esther Valentine on *The Young and the Restless*, which she has played since 1982.

Linder graduated with a BA in theatre arts from San Francisco State University. After graduation, Linder found work on television, including roles on *Archie Bunker's Place* and *Bay City Blues*.

In addition to her work on television, Linder serves as a flight attendant for United Airlines. Linder has been starring on "The Young and the Restless" for 23 years and she's also one of two Daytime Governors at the Academy of Television Arts and Sciences (ATAS), who present the Emmys. Linder is also the national spokesperson for The ALS Association (www.alsa.org) and is active with TV Cares, ATAS's AIDS fundraising and awareness organization, and the Make-a-Wish Foundation.

For her contributions in television, Linder earned a star on the Hollywood Walk of Fame, which will be installed at some point in 2008. She is the fourth actor to earn a star on the Walk of Fame solely on the merits of acting on a soap opera, after Macdonald Carey, Jeanne Cooper and 2005 honoree Susan Lucci.

Roles

- *The Young and the Restless* -Esther Valentine (Recurring: 1982 to November 1985, Contract: November 1985 to Present)
- *Bay City Blues* (1983)
- *Archie Bunker's Place* (1979)

External links

- KateLinder.com [1]
- Kate Linder's Myspace page [2]
- Kate Linder at the Internet Movie Database [3]

Tracey E. Bregman

Tracey E. Bregman	
Born	May 29, 1963 Munich, Germany
Other names	Tracy Bregman Tracey Bregman Recht Tracey E. Bregman Recht Tracy E. Bregman Recht
Occupation	Actress
Years active	1978–present
Spouse	Ronald Recht (1987-present)

Tracey E. Bregman (born May 29, 1963) is an American soap opera actress. She is best known for the role of Lauren Fenmore on *The Young and the Restless* (1983 to 1995, 2000, 2001–present) and *The Bold and the Beautiful* (1995–1999, 1992, 1993, 1994, 2002, 2004, 2007) and for her role as Sarah Smythe on *The Young and the Restless* (2010).

Personal life

She was born in Munich, Germany to American musical arranger, record producer and composer Buddy Bregman and actress Suzanne Lloyd. She lived in Great Britain until the age of 10 when her family relocated to California. She has been acting since she was 11 years old.

In 2004, Bregman launched her own yoga inspired clothing line "Bountiful Buddha" which sold popularly at friend Lisa Rinna's boutique "Belle Gray" in Los Angeles.

Bergman is also an active supporter and honorary board member for Chenoa Manor, an animal sanctuary in Chester County, Pennsylvania.[1]

As implied by her clothing line, Bergman regularly does Yoga. Her favorite novel is *The Red Tent* by Anita Diamant. Some of her favorite films are *Terms of Endearment*, *When Harry Met Sally*, Broadcast News - she has been quoted as saying that she "likes to laugh and cry in the same movie!" Television shows she has said to enjoy are *The Actors Studio on Bravo!*, *Gilmore Girls* and *Sex and the City*. Lastly, She is a big fan of the George Foreman grill.

Bregman has been married to real estate developer Ronald Recht since December 5, 1987. Bregman and Recht have two sons. She also has two stepdaughters, Emily and Lindsay, from husband Ron's previous marriage. They reside in Malibu, California.

She is good friends with her *Y&R* co-stars Michelle Stafford and Christian LeBlanc.

Career

Despite her recurring status as Lauren on *The Young and the Restless*, she continues to be featured prominently in storylines, namely in the 2005-06 storyline involving the return of her character's arch nemesis, Sheila Carter (Kimberlin Brown). Lauren has been married to lawyer Michael Baldwin, portrayed by Christian LeBlanc, since December 9, 2005. Her previous marriages and relationships include detective Paul Williams, rock star Danny Romalatti, Dr. Scott Grainger, Brad Carlton, Ridge Forrester, and Eric Forrester. Lauren has one son, Scotty Grainger Jr., with Dr. Scott Grainger who is now deceased. Although Scotty was born on screen in 1992, when he reappeared in Genoa City in 2006, he was aged to be 24 years of age - a grad student currently working on his masters in Education. The aging of Scotty appeared to be quite unrealistic as the character of Lauren is only about 40 or so, which is likely why he left the canvas of Genoa City shortly after his return. Lauren recently gave birth to a second child, Fenmore Michael Baldwin (aka "Fen"). He too was kidnapped by Sheila in February 2007, but has since been returned to his parents safe and sound.

Lauren Fenmore's parents are Neil Fenmore, played by Jim Storm, and Joanna Manning, portrayed by Susan Seaforth Hayes, best known for her role as Julie on *Days of our Lives*. She is the CEO of her late father's international chain of department stores, "Fenmore's" which is largely how she acquired her wealth. For a complete history of her character, please see the character's history page.

In light of her character's newfound romance with Christian LeBlanc's character Michael, Bregman's recognition has increased immensely due to the couple's popularity.

Prior to *The Young and the Restless*, Bregman also appeared on the soap opera Days of our Lives between the years of 1978 - 1980, portraying troubled teen Donna Temple Craig.

As of April 2010, Bregman took on the role of Sheila Carter's sister Sarah, who is in fact a double for her character Lauren.

She also appeared along side *Y&R* co-star Christian LeBlanc in the video for *I Keep On Loving You* by Reba McEntire in 2010.

She was the first actress to be awarded the Daytime Emmy Award for Outstanding Younger Actress in a Drama Series (then known as the "Outstanding Ingenue in a Drama Series") when it was introduced in 1985.

Selected filmography

Show	Character	Duration
The Young and the Restless	Lauren Fenmore Sarah Smythe	1983–1994, 1995, 2000, 2001–present April 2, 2010- May 4, 2010
Sex & Mrs. X	Katherine	2000
The Bold and the Beautiful	Lauren Fenmore	1992, 1993, 1994, 1995-1999, 2002, 2004, 2007
The Love Boat	Trish Carruthers	February 1982
Days of our Lives	Donna Temple Craig	1978–1980
Happy Birthday to Me	Ann Thomerson	1981

External links

- Tracey E. Bregman [1] at the Internet Movie Database
- Tracey E. Bregman profile from Y&R Online [2]
- [3] at Tv.com

Jess Walton

Jess Walton	
Born	February 18, 1949 Grand Rapids, Michigan, U.S.
Occupation	actress
Years active	1970 - present

Jess Walton (born February 18, 1949, Grand Rapids, Michigan) is an American actress, best known for her role as Jill Foster Abbott on the American soap opera, *The Young and the Restless*.

Early life

Born in Grand Rapids, Michigan, she attended the prestigious Loretto Abbey in Toronto. [*citation needed*] Walton left home at the age of 17 and joined a Toronto theater company. In 1969, aged 20, she moved to Hollywood.

Walton briefly dated one of the managers for Joni Mitchell and Crosby, Stills, Nash & Young, and for a time, she associated with them and other musicians, including Laura Nyro and Neil Young. In an interview, Walton recalled a memorable occasion where Nyro taught Walton and Mitchell how to belly dance. Walton says that one of the houses featured on Joni Mitchell's *Ladies of the Canyon* cover belonged to her.

In the 1970s, after signing with Universal Studios, she guest-starred on *Kojak* as a high-priced call girl. She also appeared on *The F.B.I.* and in the motorcycle movie *The Peace Killers*.

In 1980, Walton entered rehabilitation after coming to terms with a drug and alcohol addiction. [*citation needed*]

Television

After her recovery, she portrayed the role of Kelly Harper on the soap opera *Capitol*, until the show was cancelled in 1987.

Walton is perhaps best known for her portrayal of Jill Foster Abbott on the soap opera *The Young and the Restless*. She assumed the role in 1987, after prior portrayer Brenda Dickson left after an acrimonious fallout with producers. She is the fourth actress to play the part on a contract basis. Walton has been lauded for her portrayal of Jill, and is the only actress to win a Daytime Emmy Award for her work as Jill Foster Abbott. To date Walton has won two Daytime Emmy Awards for her work on *The Young and the Restless*.

Truncated filmography

- *The Young and the Restless* as Jill Abbott (June 1987 to present)
- *Capitol* as Shelly Granger/Kelly Harper (1984-1987)
- *The Streets of San Francisco* (episode "In Case Of Madness") as Lois Flynn (1976)
- *Baretta* (episode "Soldier in the Jungle") as Muriel (1976)
- *The Six Million Dollar Man* as Taneha (1975)
- *Gunsmoke* (episode, "Manolo" as Kattalin Larralde) (1975)
- *Starsky and Hutch* as Theresa (1975)
- *Kojak* (episode, "Die Before They Wake") as Cheryl Pope (1974)
- *You'll Never See Me Again* as Vicki Bliss (1973)
- *Gunsmoke* (episode, "Patricia") (1973)
- *The Peace Killers* as Kristy (1971)
- *The Strawberry Statement* as student (1970)

Personal life

Walton is married to John James, an author and grief counselor. In an interview, Walton stated that *"[B]efore [John James], I had always gone for bohemian, rock and roll types. John didn't fit the image; he was straighter."* The couple have a son, Cole (b. 1981) and reside in Sherman Oaks, California.

External links

- Jess Walton [1] at the Internet Movie Database

Peter Bergman

This article is about the soap opera actor. For the Firesign Theatre member, see Peter Bergman (comedian); for the physicist, see Peter Bergmann.

Peter Michael Bergman	
Born	June 11, 1953 Guantanamo Bay, Cuba

Peter Bergman (born June 11, 1953) is an American soap opera actor best known for his portrayals on *All My Children*, as well as *The Young and the Restless*.

Biography

The son of Walter Bergman, an American United States Navy officer, he was born in Guantanamo Bay, Cuba. Bergman was married to actress Christine Ebersole from 1976 to 1981. Since 1985, he has been married to Mariellen; with whom he has two children, Clare and Connor, who was once a five-star defensive end prospect at Harvard-Westlake School. The Bergmans currently live in California.

Career

Bergman originally auditioned for the *All My Children* casting director for the role of Dr. Jeff Martin. His first notable role was his portrayal of Dr. Cliff Warner on *All My Children*, which he played from 1979 to 1987 and again from 1988 to 1989. His character, Cliff, married Nina (Taylor Miller) four times (1980, 1982, 1986, and 1989) and divorced her three times. When the characters left the serial, their fourth marriage was intact.

In a Vicks Formula 44 cough syrup advertising campaign in 1986, Bergman told the viewing audience, "I'm not a doctor, but I play one on TV." Chris Robinson, who played Dr. Rick Webber on ABC's General Hospital, was the original spokesperson in the ad campaign, which started in 1984. Bergman replaced Robinson after the latter experienced some legal difficulties. The writer of the commercial used this opening line as a disclaimer, because the then-existing "white coat rule" prohibited people from portraying doctors in commercials without some sort of clarification/disclaimer. The original commercial with Chris Robinson became the most-recalled TV commercial in the history of the Vicks brand.

Since 1989, Bergman has played the role of Jack Abbott on *The Young and the Restless*.

In 1997, Bergman portrayed Jack Abbott in an episode "The Heather Biblow story" on The Nanny, where he shared an on-screen kiss with fellow guest-star, Pamela Anderson.

Bergman says that his success is a "series of accidents" because he didn't have huge aspirations he just wanted to be a working actor

Awards

Bergman has been nominated for Outstanding Lead Actor for his portrayal of Dr. Cliff Warner on *All My Children*.

He has been nominated 16 times (1990-2002, 2007, 2008, 2010) for his portrayal of Jack Abbott on *The Young and the Restless*.(Y&R) He won the award in 1991, 1992, and 2002. In the eighties, Bergman and fellow actor Eric Braeden had a much-publicized altercation during rehearsals. The two actors have since patched up their differences, and while they could never be described as "close friends," they are cordial in their working relationship.

Roles

- *The Young and the Restless* - Jack Abbott (1989-present)
- *The Bold and the Beautiful* - Jack Abbott (1998)
- *The Nanny* - "Himself as Jack " (1997)
- Danielle Steel's *Palamino* (1991)
- *Money, Power, Murder* - Brant (1989)
- *Fantasies* - Larry (1982)
- *All My Children* - Dr. Cliff Warner (1979-1987, 1988-1989)

See also

- Eric Braeden
- *All My Children*
- *The Young and the Restless*
- Cliff and Nina Warner
- Supercouple

External links

- Peter Bergman [1] at the Internet Movie Database
- CBS: Y&R [2]

Kristoff St. John

Kristoff St. John	
Born	July 15, 1966 New York, New York, U.S.
Other names	Cristoff St. John
Spouse	Allana Nadal (2001-2007)(*divorced*) Mia St. John (1991-1995) (*divorced*)

Kristoff St. John (born July 15, 1966 in New York City) is an American actor, best known for his role as Neil Winters on the daytime US drama *The Young and the Restless*.

Career

As a child, St. John portrayed a young Alex Haley in the ABC miniseries *Roots: The Next Generations*. He also made a small but notable appearance as Booker Brown on the ABC sitcom popular *Happy Days*, as well as a boyfriend of Denise Huxtable on an episode of *The Cosby Show*. In his first major role, he appeared as Charlie Richmond, Jr. on the CBS sitcom *Charlie & Co.*, along with Flip Wilson, Gladys Knight, and Jaleel White.

St. John's first major soap role was Adam Marshall on the NBC soap opera *Generations*, the first daytime drama to feature a core African American family from its inception. After *Generations* was cancelled in 1991, he originated the role of Neil Winters on *The Young and the Restless*, where he continues to appear to this day. A cast member for over 19 years, no African American actor has appeared on *Y&R* more frequently than St. John. In 1992, he won the Daytime Emmy Award for Outstanding Younger Actor in a Drama Series for his role in *Y&R*. Over the years, he has also won numerous NAACP Image Awards.

On September 5, 1994, he went on to host *CBS Soap Break*. The show ran until December 31, 1999.

In 2005, St. John became a special host for TV Guide Channel. In 2007, he received his fifth Daytime Emmy nomination. He was nominated for Outstanding Supporting Actor. In 2008, St. John won his second Daytime Emmy, as Outstanding Supporting Actor in a Drama Series.

He has a 6-year-old daughter Lola from last marriage to Allana Nadal. In addition, he has a son (Julian) and daughter (Paris) from his previous marriage to professional boxer Mia St. John.

Roles

- *The Cosby Show* - David James (1984)
- *Charlie & Co.* - Charlie Richmond, Jr. (1985–1986)
- *The Young and the Restless* - Neil Winters (1991–Present)
- *CBS Soap Break* - Host (1994–1999)
- *Carpool Guy* - Steven (2005)
- *Generations* - Adam Marshall (1989–1991)
- *Finish Line* - Tito Landreau (1989)
- *Pandora's Box* - Victor Dubois (2001)
- *The Champ* - Sonny (1979)
- *Big John, Little John* - Homer (1976–77)
- *The Jamie Foxx Show* - Morris (1997)
- *Family Matters* - D'Andre (1998)

Awards and nominations

- Daytime Emmy Winner, Outstanding Supporting Actor in a Drama Series (2008)
- Daytime Emmy Winner, Outstanding Younger Actor in a Drama Series (1992)
- Daytime Emmy Nomination, Outstanding Supporting Actor in a Drama Series (1999, 2000, 2007, 2008)
- Daytime Emmy Nomination, Outstanding Younger Actor in a Drama Series (1992, 1993)
- Daytime Emmy Nomination, Outstanding Supporting Actor in a Drama Series (1989; for Generations)
- Daytime Emmy Pre-Nomination, Outstanding Lead Actor (2003; for The Young and the Restless)
- Daytime Emmy Pre-Nomination, Outstanding Supporting Actor (2004, 2005)
- NAACP Image Award Winner, Outstanding Actor in a Daytime Drama Series (1991, 1992, 1993, 1994, 1995, 1996)

External links

- Kristoff St. John [1] at the Internet Movie Database

The Competition: All My Children, One Life to Live, and General Hospital

All My Children

All My Children	
Alternate titles	AMC, *All My Children: The Summer of Seduction* (summer title)
Genre	Soap opera
Creator(s)	Agnes Nixon
Senior cast member(s)	Susan Lucci Darnell Williams Michael E. Knight Debbi Morgan Walt Willey Jill Larson
Country of origin	United States
No. of episodes	10,475 (as of October 8, 2010)
Production	
Executive producer(s)	Julie Hanan Carruthers
Head writer(s)	David Kreizman Donna Swajeski
Distributor	ABC
Running time	30 minutes (1970-1977) 60 minutes (1977-present)
Broadcast	
Original channel	ABC
Original run	January 5, 1970 − present
External links	

Official website [1]

All My Children (*AMC*) is an ABC TV network soap opera that has been broadcast in the U.S., Monday through Friday since January 5, 1970; repeat episodes air weeknights on SOAPnet. Created by Agnes Nixon, the show is set in Pine Valley, Pennsylvania, a fictitious suburb of Philadelphia. Since its inception, the show has featured Susan Lucci as Erica Kane, one of daytime's most popular characters. The title of the show refers to the bonds of humanity. The poem, written by Nixon, that appears in the title credits' photo album reads:

> The Great and the Least,
> The Rich and the Poor,
> The Weak and the Strong,
> In Sickness and in Health,
> In Joy and Sorrow,
> In Tragedy and Triumph,
> You are ALL MY CHILDREN

The show title is sometimes abbreviated by fans and the press as *AMC*. The first new network daytime drama to debut in the 1970s, *All My Children* was originally owned by Creative Horizons, Inc., the company created by Nixon and her husband, Bob. The show was sold to ABC in January 1975. Originally a half-hour in length, the show expanded to an hour on April 25, 1977. Previously, the show had experimented with the hour format for one week starting on June 30, 1975, after which *Ryan's Hope* premiered.

From 1970 to 1990, *All My Children* was recorded at ABC's TV18 at 101 West 67th St, now a 50-story apartment tower. From March 1990 to December 2009, it was taped at ABC's television studio TV23 at 320 West 66th Street in Manhattan, New York City. In December 2009, the show relocated to Los Angeles and is now produced in Stages 1 and 2 at the Andrita Studios. It was confirmed on August 4, 2009 that *All My Children* and *One Life to Live* would go HD. *All My Children* started filming in High Definition on January 4, 2010 and began airing in High Definition on February 3, 2010. *All My Children* is the third soap opera to be produced and broadcast in High Definition.

At one time, the program's popularity positioned it as the most widely-recorded television show in the United States. Also, in a departure from societal norms at the time, *All My Children*, in the mid-1970s, had an audience that was estimated to be 30% male. The show ranked #1 in the daytime Nielsen ratings in the 1978-79 season. Throughout most of the 1980s and into the early 1990s, *All My Children* was the #2 daytime soap opera on the air. For the first time since 1994-1995 season *All My Children* ranked in the top three on Nielsen ratings for the week of June 28-July 2, 2010.

History

With the death of core cast member Ruth Warrick in January 2005, and the retirement of Ray MacDonnell in 2010, Susan Lucci is the only original cast member remaining on the show.

1970s

Main article: All My Children (1970-1979)

In the 1960s Agnes Nixon, then head writer for *The Guiding Light*, tried to sell a property called *All My Children* to NBC, then CBS, then NBC again through the auspices of sponsor Procter & Gamble. Despite her success and sponsor support, it was not until the start of 1970 that her brainchild finally aired. Rosemary Prinz was signed on to be the "special guest star" for six months, playing the role of liberal Amy Tyler. Prinz was well-known for her role on *As the World Turns* in the 1950s and 1960s and she was added to the show to give it an initial boost due to her name value.

Nixon strove to create a soap that was topical, and could illustrate social issues for the audience. She wanted this and a combination of regular humor for the series. To keep the action more real, she allowed the audience to locate her fictional "Pine Valley" on a map: situated just outside of Philadelphia, it was a mere hour-long train ride from New York City. However, it is not until the 1980s that it is revealed that Pine Valley is actually in Pennsylvania.

From 1970 and into the 1980s, the show was either written by Nixon herself or by her protégé, Wisner Washam. He was groomed by Nixon to take the reins in the 1980s while she focused on other endeavors, like creating and launching *Loving* in 1983.

The show's first action takes place around several families and characters. Phoebe Tyler (Ruth Warrick), who fashions herself as "Queen of Pine Valley", is the definition of a rich snob when she is introduced. A single mother, Mona Kane (Frances Heflin), and her prima donna daughter, Erica (Susan Lucci) are also introduced. Contrasting this is the stable Martin Family, headed by patriarch Joe and later (after the death of her husband, Ted Brent) by matriarch Ruth, who becomes a symbolic foundation of *All My Children*.

With Phoebe as the "Queen of Pine Valley", Erica is the "Princess". Destined to break up the young romance of classmates Tara Martin (Karen Lynn Gorney) and Phil Brent (Richard Hatch), Erica finds out that Phil is not Ruth's son but the son of Ruth's sister, Amy (Rosemary Prinz). In a selfish attempt to break up Phil and Tara, she tells everyone the truth.

All My Children's first success was its telling of young love. ABC wanted a soap opera that would bring in young viewers, and slowly the program was accomplishing that. The show's ratings did not start out strong, however. In its first year on the air, it ranked #17 out of 19 soap operas. Despite this, its audience was building with each passing year.

The show was unique for its use of the Vietnam War. Before *All My Children* debuted, no show had discussed the war in any depth. There was the character of Phoebe, a conservative, and Amy, a free-spirited liberal, both butting heads over the war, with Amy often leading protests around Pine Valley. When the character of Amy leaves, Ruth takes over as the anti-war voice. Her early 1970s protest speech wins Mary Fickett the first ever Emmy Award given to a soap opera performer back in 1972. Later in the show's run, Phoebe becomes more liberal.

In 1973, Erica Kane makes the decision to have an abortion, which becomes the first abortion aired on television. What makes the abortion particularly controversial is Erica's reason for doing it; she does not have it because her health is in jeopardy, but rather because she does not want to gain weight and lose her modeling job. The abortion story received much media attention, especially since *Roe v. Wade* had been decided just a few months before the story began airing. Within the story, Erica develops a potentially fatal infection after having the abortion, and the switch-boards at ABC lit up with calls from doctors and nurses, offering their medical opinions on how best to treat the character's case.

Phoebe's husband Charles (Hugh Franklin) gets close to Mona (Erica's mother) and his secretary at the hospital. The two fall in love and Charles divorces Phoebe, even though she tries to blackmail Mona and even fakes paralysis. In the end, Phoebe is left a drunken divorcée and Mona becomes the new Mrs. Tyler. This ordeal starts the long-time Phoebe/Mona rivalry.

When Eileen Letchworth, who portrayed Margo Flax Martin, contemplated a facelift, she talked it over with Nixon. Not only was Letchworth going to need time off, she was going to look significantly different when she returned to the show. Nixon approved and worked the facelift into a storyline. Margo wanted to impress the somewhat younger Paul Martin (William Mooney). Margo's facelift in 1974 became one of the first major storylines on television discussing cosmetic surgery and its psychological effects.

In June 1976, the character of Brooke English shows up on her Aunt Phoebe's doorstep and soon after clashes with Erica over Tom Cudahy and Mark Dalton. Since then, Brooke ends up with several of Erica's left-over men. In 1976, the show introduces fan favorite Myrtle Lum Fargate (Eileen Herlie).

By the late 1970s, the show had risen to the top of the ratings. One reason for the rise was the arrival of teenage prostitute Donna Beck. Her relationship with the handsome Dr. Chuck Tyler breathed life into the show and captivated fans. Other new additions are the arrivals of aristocratic Palmer Cortlandt (aka Peter Cooney) (James Mitchell), his somewhat creepy housekeeper Myra Murdock, and his overprotected daughter Nina (Taylor Miller), who, to Palmer's chagrin, entrances Dr. Cliff Warner (Peter Bergman). Palmer does everything in his power to break up the couple, including telling Nina she is going blind due to her diabetes. Palmer teams up with Cliff's past flame, nurse Sybil Thorne (Linda Gibboney), who confronts Cliff about fathering her son, but this is temporary; Sybil is accidentally killed by Sean Cudahy (Alan Dysert). During the murder trial, Nina is astonished to learn that her mother, Daisy Cortlandt (Gillian Spencer), whom she believes to be dead, is, in fact, alive and living in Pine Valley as 'Monique Jonville'. To complete everyone's shock, Myra acknowledges that Daisy is her daughter. *All My Children* also found memorable villains in Billy Clyde Tuggle and Ray Gardner.

1980s

The early '80s is considered to have been a "golden period" for the show and the "Golden Age" for supercouples. Younger characters, such as Greg Nelson and Jenny Gardner (Laurence Lau and Kim Delaney), Liza Colby (Marcy Walker), Liza's best friend Amanda (Amanda Bearse), Jesse Hubbard and Angie Baxter (Darnell Williams and Debbi Morgan) and a now-grown-up Tad Martin (Michael E. Knight), who was now legally Ruth and Joe's son, enter the scene.

The storyline involving Liza plotting to win Greg back after he leaves her for Jenny became a fan favorite, as was the Greg and Jenny and Jesse and Angie pairings. The legend of "Tad the Cad" is born when Tad takes Liza's virginity, then simultaneously begins having sex with her mother, socialite Marian Colby (Jennifer Bassey), who eventually is sent to prison and returns to marry Stuart Chandler (David Canary). Powerful businessman Adam Chandler and his twin brother Stuart become significant Pine Valley residents. This is the first arrival of members of the Chandler family.

Jesse and Jenny's summer in New York City became regarded as one of the greatest storylines in the history of the series. For older appeal, Jenny and Tad's natural mother Opal (Dorothy Lyman) was also added to the canvas, where she opens the Glamorama salon and spa. Opal greatly showcased *All My Children*'s attempt at humor and satire.

The character of Erica begins to take on a larger-than-life role by the 1980s. This is evident with her writing an autobiography, "Raising Kane", and turning it into a motion picture. When her presumed half-sister Silver (Deborah Goodrich) accuses her of murdering Kent Bogard (Michael Woods, Lee Goodart), her former lover and boss, she goes on the run, fleeing to the Hollywood Hills. She does this all while posing as a nun. Her forest encounter with a grizzly bear after she escapes a kidnapping attempt made by Adam is considered a memorable moment. The character goes on to marry over 10 times (with her most recent wedding taking place in May 2005).

The show made their first attempt at tackling the taboo topic of homosexuality in 1983. Tricia Pursley portrayed the divorced Devon McFadden, who believes she is falling in love with her psychiatrist, Lynn Carson (portrayed by Donna Pescow). Lynn admits to being a lesbian, and Devon admits her crush. No other American soap opera had done a story about homosexuality.

The show intelligently tackled the issue of drug use when Mark La Mura's character, Mark Dalton, becomes addicted to cocaine after years of casual use. His half-sister, Erica, stages an intervention with his friends to have him confront his problems. They practice a "tough love" policy that has Mark admit to the addiction. The informative episode showed how to hold an intervention, and the stages to go through for a successful confrontation.

Controversy was prompted in 1987 with the arrival of Cindy Parker (Ellen Wheeler), who would later fall in love with Stuart. The character was revealed to have AIDS. Through visits by Dr. Angie Hubbard, the show educated the public on how the disease was spread and how to prevent it. Cindy had contracted HIV from her husband, Fred, who contracted it from sharing needles for drug use. Cindy is attacked by a vigilante hate group led by her niece, Skye Chandler. The tragedy of the attack shows the extremes of violence that occur everyday to victims of the disease. Cindy marries Stuart and he adopts her son, Scott. She dies early in 1989 in one of the show's most watched episodes.

By 1989, ABC wanted changes at *All My Children*. The show was getting about 6.5 million viewers per episode, but there sentiment that the program had lost its unique sense of humor. Nixon and Wisner Washam, who had both written the show since the '70s, were faced with a merry-go-round of executive producers, starting in the mid-'80s when producer Jacqueline Babbin left. Jorn Winther was hired to executive produce the show. Efforts were made to bring the show back to the glory days of the late '70s and early '80s. This would mean adding a mixture of *both* social issues and also the intelligent satire that the show had been known for.

Felicia Minei Behr was hired as the new executive producer in early 1989. Having been a producer on Ryan's Hope, Behr was familiar with *All My Children*, having been an associate producer from 1970 to 1975. Behr welcomed the input of both Nixon and Washam. To Nixon, the show finally had a stable executive producer. Behr worked with Nixon and Washam, crafting a baby storyline involving the characters of Adam, Brooke, Tad, and Dixie (Cady McClain). By this time, the show had also found a "hit couple" in Cecily and Nico (portrayed by Rosa Nevin and Maurice Benard), but Behr was unable to convince either to remain with the show, and the duo left at the end of 1989.

ABC was pleased with Behr; Nixon was as well, and decided her creation was safe in the hands of the new producer. Behr, however, made the unpopular decision to fire Peter Bergman (Cliff Warner) during this time, as well as Ellen Wheeler (Karen) and Robert Gentry (Ross Chandler). Bergman's departure was particularly frustrating to Debbi Morgan (who thought it was a cop-out by ABC on the promising interracial Angie/Cliff pairing; Morgan later defected to the new NBC soap *Generations* in protest), Taylor Miller (who was misled when Behr approached her to bring back her character Nina; Miller was frustrated to find out she had only been brought back for two weeks to facilitate Bergman's departure: Cliff and Nina reunited, married yet again, and left Pine Valley, leaving Miller to lament to *Soap Opera Digest* that she felt it was going backward for both characters, and difficult emotionally to play), and Bergman himself (who had just bought a house, and was left without a paycheck, unexpectedly). Behr then brought back fan favorite Opal Gardner, but instead of contacting Emmy winner Dorothy Lyman to reprise the role, Behr hired Jill Larson. Lyman later noted her disappointment in never being contacted about reprising the role. Behr also brought back Billy Clyde Tuggle (the former pimp who first made his big splash in the '70s), only to kill him off for good.

1990s

At the time of Behr's hiring in early 1989, the show usually ranked around #4 in the ratings. By 1990, the show had inched up to the #3 spot. Billy Clyde Tuggle returns to Pine Valley in 1990, after a ten-year absence (in prison). He proceeds to undo the lives of many in Pine Valley. He tells his daughter, Emily Ann Sago, that he is her natural father, devastating her with the truth that she was the product of rape. He dies tumbling over a bridge (with Tad Martin), ending the reign of one of Pine Valley's most evil and entertaining characters ever.

ABC chose Megan McTavish, a former actress who had been on the writing team since 1987, to be its new head writer. She was promoted to head writer in 1992, with Nixon serving as Executive Head Writer. Stories such as Molly's leukemia, Ceara Connor (Genie Frances') incest, Mona's lung cancer, and Deconstruction (a story about racism), were all praised in soap opera magazines for their social conscience. Other storylines included the 'Who Killed Will?' mystery, Willow Lake Acres (a both humorous and serious tale about the plight of the elderly in a fraudulent nursing home), and a tornado that rocked Pine Valley. Behr also helped craft a story re-exploring Erica's father, Eric Kane. It was revealed he had faked his own death. In a comical twist, Erica finds him working as a clown in a traveling circus. This is yet one of the several re-writes during *All My Children* post-1990 that frustrated and irritated fans. The audience soon learns that Erica was raped on her 14th birthday, by her father's actor friend Richard Fields. She became pregnant and gave the baby up for adoption to the Harts, a couple from Florida. Years later, the child, Kendall Hart (Sarah Michelle Gellar, Alicia Minshew), emerges and makes her way to Pine Valley after finding out her biological mother is the famous Erica Kane, to wreak havoc on her and assume her glamorous lifestyle, which she feels is her birth right. Erica had thought she had put that whole nightmare behind her, only to have it come back years later with a vengeance and a name. Mother and daughter loath one another during this time within the series. The introduction of Kendall is a major retcon, but still a popular story. The Santos, Dillon, Frye, and Keefer families were introduced during this time as well.

The Tad and Dixie pairing had become especially popular. The show also had other couples with large followings during this time: Dimitri and Erica (Michael Nader), Trevor (James Kiberd) and Natalie (Kate Collins), and Hayley (Kelly Ripa) and Brian (Gregory Gordon, Matt Borlengthi, Brian L. Greene).

By the early-mid-1990s, some of McTavish's storytelling received criticism for being gimmick-driven (i.e. multiple dual roles, bomb plots). Reports soon surfaced that Behr and McTavish were having conflicts about storylines and the direction of the series. After the O.J. Simpson trial preempted daytime television programs throughout late 1994 and into 1995, many soaps saw their ratings decline, and *All My Children* was no different. When Megan McTavish was fired from her head writing post in the spring, former head writer Lorraine Broderick was tapped by Behr to lead the team once again.

Broderick's tenure under Behr was popular among critics and fans for returning *All My Children* to its socially relevant, character-driven roots. Her most significant successes were Erica's drug addiction story (with the character receiving treatment at the Betty Ford Center), and also the story of homophobia over a gay high school boy and a history teacher. However, with the ratings still stagnant, ABC fired longtime executive producer Felicia Minei Behr, and brought in Francesca James (who had previously won an Emmy award acting on the show as twins Kitty and Kelly). The storylines now included a voodoo arc with the popular Noah and Julia (Keith Hamilton Cobb and Sydney Penny), a fantasy story for Myrtle featuring the "real" Santa Claus, and finally a baby kidnapping story involving Erica.

Despite winning three consecutive Daytime Emmys for writing during her tenure on *All My Children*, Broderick was replaced in December 1997 by her predecessor, McTavish. The first major story McTavish tackled was, "ironically", one created by Broderick, Bianca Montgomery's anorexia. The character of Bianca, Erica's young daughter, is checked into a facility to treat the disease. Apart from the anorexia story, McTavish's tales were plot-driven and made implausible alterations to the show's history such as the resurrection of Erica's lifetime-love, Mike Roy (Nicholas Surovy). In 1998, the show again got a new executive producer, Jean Dadario Burke, taking over from Francesca James. She would become known to many speculating fans as a weak producer with little vision.

Cady McClain, who had left the show as Dixie in 1996, returned to the delight of her fans, but other storylines — involving ghosts, poison tattoos, Nazi art, and a sperm switch — were all ill-received. By the start of 1999, with *All My Children* being voted as the "Worst of 1998" by *Soap Opera Digest*, McTavish was once again fired.

As ratings began to fall in the late 1990s, ABC convinced Nixon to make a brief return. Many long-running actors, such as Michael Nader, James Kiberd, and Robin Mattson, left their roles.

2000s

Nixon decided to write a story that would rejuvenate the show and be socially relevant at the same time. This resulted in the series revealing Erica's daughter Bianca as a lesbian. Within the series, Bianca admits the truth to her mother in December 2000. Though initially controversial, the storyline was praised by fans and critics. Bianca emerged as a breakout character and lesbian icon. The show found additional success in the pairing of newcomers Leo and Greenlee (Josh Duhamel and Rebecca Budig).

Richard Culliton wrote several of *All My Children's* early 2000s storylines. He created popular characters Frankie and Maggie Stone, and said Frankie was already intended to be killed in a murder storyline after only three months on the series. Culliton and ABC executives were surprised when viewers became attached to the romance between Bianca and Frankie, developed by Culliton with Frankie's debut. These fans attributed Frankie's death to the show's fear to focus on a lesbian romance. Eventually, Culliton introduced the idea to bring back popular actress Elizabeth Hendrickson, who had portrayed Frankie, as Frankie's twin sister Maggie. Culliton continued to write for the show until late 2002.

After more staff turnover in recent years, McTavish again returned as head writer. Her storylines began airing in July 2003, which included the controversial rape of Bianca. Gone upon McTavish's latest return was Jean Dadario Burke as executive producer, being replaced with Julie Hanan Carruthers.

Under McTavish, ratings fluctuated back and forth. To lure back long-time viewers, McTavish created new characters and romances, as well as scripted the return of various characters who had been gone for long periods of time. She introduced star-crossed couple JR Chandler and Babe Carey upon writing JR's return to the series, scripted most of popular pairing Bianca Montgomery and Maggie Stone's love story, and created fellow popular couple Zach Slater and Kendall Hart. Julia Santos (Sydney Penny) and Janet Dillon (Kate Collins, who was originally slated to return for a brief stint) were eventually given contracts.

On July 26, 2006, Tanika Ray, Jonathan Aldridge, and pop star Rihanna appeared on the show. During the Rihanna appearance, a controversial storyline involving Erica's thought-to-be-aborted son having come to Pine Valley under the name Josh Madden intensifies when Josh learns of how he truly came to exist. In August 2006, after months of speculation, it was confirmed that fan favorite Eden Riegel would be reprising her Emmy winning role as Bianca. She was a part of a controversial storyline centered on transgender character Zarf/Zoe. Since departing the show in February 2005, Riegel has continued to return to the series for limited guest appearances.

The most notable return was Cady McClain's return as show heroine Dixie Cooney Martin. The news of her return spread just two weeks before she reappeared on the series. In an unpopular and controversial move by the series, the writers chose to kill off Dixie in January 2007 only a year after her return. The character's death was the result of the Satin Slayer storyline where she is unintentionally murdered in place of character Babe Carey.

Another prominent return to the series occurred on February 9, 2007, when Susan Pratt returned as Barbara Montgomery. Pratt made her last appearance in July of that year. That same month, McTavish was fired as head writer, reportedly due to viewer criticism about her storylines. On May 21, 2007, James Harmon Brown and Barbara Esensten were announced as the new head writers of *All My Children*. The duo wrote for *Days of our Lives*, *One Life to Live*, *Dynasty* and *Port Charles*, and created and wrote for *The City*.

On December 12, 2007, ABC revealed Rebecca Budig would be returning to the series as Greenlee Smythe; the return was one of the most widely reported in daytime television history, attracting mainstream media attention such as the *Associated Press* and *New York Daily News*. Budig's return was overshadowed by controversy when news of Sabine Singh's reportedly unfair treatment as a Greenlee recast in order to bring Budig back incited viewer outrage.

On December 25, 2007, *Soap Opera Digest* reported the return of fan favorites Debbi Morgan and Darnell Williams as Jesse Hubbard and Angie Baxter. Morgan returned on January 18, 2008, and Williams on January 25, 2008. In April 2008, it was announced that Laurence Lau would briefly reprise the role of Greg Nelson for Jesse and Angie's much anticipated wedding.

On May 21, 2008, Charles Pratt, Jr., former co-head writer for *General Hospital*, was announced as a replacement for Brown and Esensten amid record low ratings.

On November 6, 2008, *All My Children* aired a special episode in which veterans share their stories unscripted.

On November 12, 2008, the show celebrated its 10,000th show with a special appearance by Nixon and a special tribute to Myrtle Fargate (as portrayed by Eileen Herlie). On December 19, 2008, a special episode ran for Herlie, showing clips from the past.

On February 16, 2009, *All My Children* made daytime history with the nuptials of Reese Williams and Bianca Montgomery, the first legal same-sex marriage in American daytime television.

On November 20, 2009, Pratt was fired as head writer. Daytime Emmy-winning former head writer Lorraine Broderick was brought back to lead the writing team on an interim basis. Reportedly, Broderick returned at the request of show creator Agnes Nixon, but was not interested in remaining permanently as the team's top scribe.

2010s

On January 5, 2010, *All My Children* celebrated its 40th anniversary with an episode structured like a documentary and hosted by character Hayley Santos. It featured appearances by characters Palmer Cortlandt, Nina Warner, Maria Santos Grey, Brooke English, Greg Nelson, Bianca Montgomery, Mateo Santos, and Lily Montgomery. It was also the final episode for characters Joe and Ruth Martin, who are moving to Florida for retirement, and the final appearance for Palmer, as his portrayer James Mitchell, died just over two weeks after the episode's airing.

On January 13, 2010, ABC Daytime announced the appointment of David Kreizman and Donna Swajeski as the co-head writers of *All My Children*, replacing interim head writer Lorraine Broderick, who in turn replaced the fan-reviled Charles Pratt, Jr.. Brian Frons, head of ABC daytime, stated, "David and Donna are the perfect team to bring new ideas to *All My Children* while remaining true to its core by telling stories with a focus on the integrity of the show's history, its characters and families on the canvas." Prior to his appointment on *All My Children*, Kriezman was the head writer of *Guiding Light* from 2004 to the show's cancellation in 2009 and the co-head writer of *As the World Turns* since 2009. Swajeski's prior experience includes a head writing stint on *Another World* from 1988 to 1992.

With the death on January 22 of James Mitchell (Palmer Cortlandt 1979-2010), the show aired a tribute episode to Palmer on Tuesday April 20, 2010. Gillian Spencer (Daisy Murdoch Cortlandt), Taylor Miller (Nina Cortlandt) and Cady McClain (Dixie Cooney Martin) returned for the episode.

On February 8, Walt Willey returned as a contract cast member in the role of Jackson Montgomery, following numerous months away and dispute about his future on the show. On February 23, Julia Barr reprised the role of Brooke English; Brooke's return was timed to the retirement of David Canary (Adam Chandler) after more than 26 years on the show. Their final episode aired April 23, 2010.

On July 18, 2010 All My Children lost one of its original cast members Larry Keith. Larry was on the show from 1970-2005. Larry portrayed Nick Davis who gave Erica Kane the nickname "Princess". He was last seen on January 5, 2005 for All My Children's 35th anniversary episode. There have been no plans announced to the public if or when a tribute episode will be done.

In September 2010, Daytime Emmy winner Vincent Irizzary's character, the popular villain David Hayward, was murdered. There is much speculation as to whether or not the actor willingly left the show or if he was fired. On September 16, 2010, Adam Mayfield (Scott Chandler) and Brittany Allen (Marissa Tasker) were announced to be leaving the show. ABC reports that they wanted to take both the characters in a different direction involving the Annie/JR/Marissa/Scott storyline. They are both expected to air until late October 2010.

On September 22, 2010 it was announced that Daniel Cosgrove (ex-Scott, AMC; ex-Bill, GL; ex-Chris, ATWT) will return to AMC and replace Adam Mayfield (Scott) as Scott Chandler. His return will be sometime in December.

Title sequences

All title sequences use a book of the show's title. Ever since the debut in 1970, AMC's opener has included a photo album/scrapbook in some kind of form.

January 5, 1970 - December 29, 1989 [2]
January 2, 1990 - January 2, 1995 [2]
January 3, 1995 - October 4, 2002 [2]
October 7, 2002 - May 28, 2004 [2]
May 31, 2004–present [2]

The First Two Decades With the premiere, the sequence was simple: a camera slowly zooms in on a leather-bound photo album as a female hand enters the image to open the album. On the first page of the album, the title is shown in calligraphic type. Until at least June 1970, the hand turned to a second page, crediting Rosemary Prinz as a "Special Guest Star". Prinz, at the time, was the cast member with the most experience in soaps, and crediting her in the sequence was used as a way to coax her fans to tune in. She left after six months on the show, and the second page was eliminated from the sequence.

In June 1970, the sequence was updated, featuring the same hand-turning the book format, only now based on a larger table/credenza, and the book was more centered. The title appeared in the same calligraphic font, but the inside title page now revealed a painted spring of flowers to accompany it. The hand would begin to turn to the next page just as the sequence faded out, to give the effect of someone displaying a full family photo album. However, additional pages would never be seen again during the run of this sequence.

This set ran for twenty years, making it one of the longest-running packages in soap history. The theme music used with this sequence was written by Dina Dore and her daughter Carlina Paul. It went through two principal arrangements; in the beginning it was a soft lullaby-type tune. Retained from the 1970 sequence, it ran through 1971. Another version debuted in late 1971 and was used until 1976. A new version of the theme, more sweeping and cheery than the two previous versions, and featuring full orchestration by Jack Urbont, was used from 1976 to 1989. The last and final episode of *All My*

Children with the "title inside page" sequence aired on December 29, 1989.

The Falling Photographs In 1989 executive producer Felicia Minei Behr decided to create a new sequence to bring AMC into the 1990s for the 20th Anniversary. Billy Barber and Bob Israel were hired to record the new theme. By the middle of December 1989 the recording of the theme music was completed. Then, all contract cast members of the show were all called to do a photoshoot and once the filming was completed, animation began. The animation was completed early in the last week of December and by December 29 the sequence was complete. The new sequence debuted during the 20th Anniversary week in January 1990. This new sequence kept the photo album theme, but expanded upon it. It began with the camera panning across a desk featuring framed pictures of longtime cast members.

This dissolved into a series of animations in which still pictures of each cast member hovered into piles on the desk. It ended with a portrait of lead actress Susan Lucci slowly sliding onto a page in the photo album, as it closed to reveal the title in an Old English type on the cover. Occasionally, the title would disappear from the cover and a sponsor's logo would be in its place, with the announcer doing an ad for the sponsor.

As popular as the sequence was, the theme music was even more popular. Written by Billy Barber, it began with a perky melody. A slightly remixed / remastered version of this theme debuted in December 1992 with a quieter, slower arrangement at the beginning.

The last episode of *AMC* with the falling pictures sequence aired on January 2, 1995.

The Locket and Pearls In 1994, Behr decided to come up with another new sequence for the 25th Anniversary. She hired saxophonist David Benoit to record the theme and then decided she wanted heirlooms such as necklaces, chess pieces, and different exteriors. By Christmas Eve 1994, she decided that they would include motion backgrounds, not in color however, to make the opening a tour of Pine Valley and finalized most of the components such as cast pictures. On December 29, 1994, the sequence was completed with motion images. However, they became stills due to budgets. For the 25th Anniversary week, the new sequence made its debut. The first episode of *AMC* with the locket sequence aired on January 4, 1995. It featured stills of each cast member fading in and out of a white background while various images, including galloping horses, house exteriors, pearl necklaces, and pink roses, crossfaded throughout the cast images. Susan Lucci was again given a nod as her picture was always first, and was the only one in the sequence to be framed with a silver frame. Finally, Agnes Nixon's hand-written epigram for the show crossfaded in the background just as the photo album did.

On March 8, 1995, a new arrangement of this theme debuted to replace the January 1995 version; it was shortened at the beginning and lengthened towards the end with a few new instruments. Also, a new quiet piano arrangement debuted on April 4, 1995. In October 1995, the sequence was updated to include posed images of most cast members, but the images were still motionless. In July 1996 the opening was updated and debuted live video images of the former stills. In August 1997, the aforementioned piano arrangement became the main title theme. It was mixed differently from 1995 format(including a harp) and debuted in September 1997 with a thoroughly updated cast montage which lasted to October 1998 when a new upbeat version that included the ending version would debut. The upbeat cut debuted in January 1999. In 2000 it was remixed with a few additional instrument tracks included, and used Digital Surround Sound. All of the music that accompanied these sequences were composed by David Benoit. *AMC* retired this sequence on October 4, 2002.

The Scrapbook On October 7, 2002, after nearly eight years of the previous sequence, a new one made its debut. The first *AMC* episode with the Scrapbook opening aired on October 7, 2002. It featured the photo album, but unlike the other sequences, the photo album was constantly seen throughout. It began with a closeup of the album (with the title on the cover) as it opened. The Agnes Nixon epigram is seen on the front page, but the screen fades into the montage of cast member images, all done in live action. The photos were already on their pages in the album and as each face was shown, the name of the character was scrawled on their page in the book, similar to what many people do with their own family scrapbooks. Yet again, Susan Lucci is paid homage by being at the end of both formats of this sequence. This time, however, she shared that honor with David Canary, as he was in both sequences as well, as Adam Chandler in one and Stuart in the other. The theme that accompanied this sequence was a much-loved update of the 1990-1995 theme originally composed by Billy Barber, this time with contributions by Robert Israel. There were two music versions of this sequence, the first of which was a quiet, fast tempo that lasted for two weeks when it was replaced by a more dramatic theme. An alternate theme debuted in 2003 and was used occasionally until 2004.

The Family Album After barely a year and a half of the previous opening, the show debuted another on May 31, 2004. This opening was styled after the commercial break bumpers that were present on all of ABC's serials at the time. *One Life to Live* and *General Hospital's* openings were done in similar ways to the *All My Children* opening. The theme music was a considerable remix of the previous version, with a revised intro, a percussion track, and electric guitar track added.

The new opening generated mixed opinions from the audience. The pros of it were that many pictures from the show's past, including montages of classic Susan Lucci and Ruth Warrick headshots and a wedding portrait from Edmund and Maria's 1994 wedding, was seen at the beginning. Also in favor was the updated version of the classic early 1990s theme song. Cons were Ryan's image was after Erica's, which many felt that place belonged to Alicia Minshew's Kendall. The All My Children book letter font was in Monotype Corsiva rather than the traditional Old English Text and the book was in a different red hue. This was also the first time that the show's name was written on a single line, as opposed to the usual three lines. In December 2006, a slightly modified version of the theme debuted and is still in use.

Closing Credits[2] For the first 12 years of *All My Children*, the closing credits used the format of a single mimed scene of one or more characters engaging in an activity or interacting with each other, usually only on a single set. Credits would always scroll over the scene, and would feature the full cast list after production principals on some days, while a full crew list would appear on others.

Occasionally, as is still the case to this very day, full cast and crew would run if enough time allotted. As with most soaps, this entire credit list was known for running especially on holiday episodes.

During the entire time *All My Children* used mimed scenes for the closings, thin, regular Craw Clarendon font, in white, was used. In the era in which the show debuted, this font was commonly used on two other ABC soaps, *General Hospital* and *One Life to Live*. *OLTL* was also an Agnes Nixon production, under her Creative Horizons company, which explains the similar cosmetic look between that soap and *All My Children*. *GH*, however, had been completely purchased by ABC come the early 1970s, but had always used Craw Clarendon Condensed font as opposed to the regular variant of the type utilized on *OLTL* and *AMC*. Both programs saw their closing sequence formats go unchanged even after Ms. Nixon sold them to ABC entirely, in 1975. By 1978, the Craw Clarendon used on *AMC* became smaller and thinly embossed, but by that same year the program was the only one still using the font, as *OLTL*'s credit setup changed at that time. It should also be noted that beginning in the late 1970s, the scrolling cast list went from being completely centered to displaying character names on the left side of the screen, while actors' names were positioned on the right. Copyright notice first appeared on *AMC* in 1980; it appeared in small Arial font under the "Videotaped at ABC Television Center in New York" credit until 1982.

In mid-1982, *AMC* experienced its first major credits overhaul. The credits went from running on an image frame to being computer generated, and for a few months, remained in Craw Clarendon font. The Arial-set copyright continued, but was now under a closing display of the show's title. That fall, following Jacqueline Babbin's arrival as executive producer, the font setup entirely changed to Brittanica Bold for actors and crew members, and small Helvetica for character names and production titles. Subsequently, the cast list now scrolled completely on the left hand side. *All My Children* became the first ABC daytime program to then implement a network-mandated copyright, set in a variation of italicized Century Gothic font. This copyright had been introduced on all ABC News programs, daytime and nighttime, a couple of years earlier. With the introduction of this notice format, "All Rights Reserved" was added to the copyright for the first time, and it originally contained the word "Copyright" before the symbol; it would be removed by early 1984. This mandate subsequently made its way to all other ABC daytime programs in the next year and a half (with the exception of *General Hospital*, which has traditionally been allowed different credit and branding practices by ABC).

Thereafter, *AMC*'s credits continued to see periodic alterations, especially with the changing of the guard in executive producers. By 1985, the credit portions in Britannica Bold became smaller and super-embossed with black shadowing. The "Videotaped At" credit went from being entirely in Helvetica to having the first line be in the latter font, with the next two lines appearing in Britannica Bold. In early 1988, the cast list reverted to running centered on the screen, for the first time since the late 1970s. Not long after Felicia Minei Behr became the new executive producer in early 1989, black shadowing on the credits was toned down. For the first time in *AMC*s 19-year history, the closing visuals changed; they now featured stills of scenes from that day's episode (a practice Ms. Behr kept during the final months of *Ryan's Hope*, as well as what was currently seen on *Loving*). These latest changes lasted into the second-generation visuals package that premiered in January 1990. In 1991, the still-shots were replaced by live-action repeats of select scenes aired in the given episode.

In late 1995, most closing credit sequences became carded in groups over the live-action shots. On the final week of January 1996, a new network-mandated sequence took over, as they did on all other ABC soaps. The font was switched from the long-running Brittanica/Helvetica combo to Windsor type, and ran just as they did in the last few months prior to the change. The early-1980s style ABC copyright notice was also retired in favor of a new, three-line formatted notice, in a more new-age variation of Helvetica. "Copyright (year)" was on the top line, "American Broadcasting Companies, Inc." was on the middle, and "All Rights Reserved" was below. Later in 1996, the ABC Go Network web logo was added above the closing title display, and in 1997, episode stills returned to the credits.

It should also be noted that for several years during the 1980s, the *All My Children* episodes that officially commemorated Christmas ran the entire credit setup (cast and crew) entirely in Brittanica Bold, sans the use of the accompanying Helvetica. All credits would be centered, including the cast, even during the years in which the cast appeared to the left of the screen, usually. Once the Felicia Minei Behr era began, long Christmas credits utilized the year-round Brittanica/Helvetica combo.

Cast and characters

Main article: List of All My Children cast members

See also: List of All My Children characters

See also: List of All My Children miscellaneous characters

See also: Children of All My Children

Ratings

For historical ratings information, see List of US daytime soap opera ratings

1970s ratings

1969-1970 season

- 1. *As the World Turns* 13.6
- 17. *All My Children* 4.4 (Debut)

1970-1971 season

- 1. *As the World Turns* 12.4
- 17. *All My Children* 4.8

1971-1972 season

- 1. *As the World Turns* 11.1
- 17. *All My Children* 5.7

1972-1973 season

- 1. *As the World Turns* 10.6
- 8. *All My Children* 8.2 (Tied with The Guiding Light)

1973-1974 season

- 1. *As the World Turns* 10.6 (Tied with Days of our Lives and Another World)
- 6. *All My Children* 9.1

1974-1975 season

- 1. *As the World Turns* 10.8
- 5. *All My Children* 9.3

1975-1976 season

- 1. *As the World Turns* 9.4
- 6. *All My Children* 8.1 (Tied with Guiding Light)

1976-1977 season

- 1. *As the World Turns* 9.9
- 6. *All My Children* 8.2

1977-1978 season

- 1. *As the World Turns* 8.6 (Tied with Another World)
- 3. *All My Children* 8.4

1978-1979 Season (HH Ratings)

- 1. *All My Children* 9.0
- 6. *One Life to Live* 8.0

1980s ratings

1979-1980 Season (HH Ratings) (Nielsen)

- 1. *General Hospital* 9.9
- 2. *All My Children* 9.2

1980-1981 Season (HH Ratings) (Nielsen)

- 1. *General Hospital* 11.4
- 2. *All My Children* 9.1 (Tied with One Life to Live)

1981-1982 Season (HH Ratings)

- 1. *General Hospital* 11.2
- 2. *All My Children* 9.4

Highest rated week in daytime history (Week of November 16-November 20, 1981) (HH ratings)

- 1. *General Hospital* 16.0 (3-4pm)
- 2. *All My Children* 10.2 (1-2pm) (#2 in viewers)
- 2. *One Life to Live* 10.2 (2-3pm) (#3 in viewers)
- 4. *Guiding Light* 7.4 (3-4pm)
- 5. *The Young and the Restless* 7.0 (12:30-1:30pm)

1982-1983 Season

- 1. *General Hospital* 9.8
- 2. *All My Children* 9.4

1983-1984 Season

- 1. *General Hospital* 10.0
- 2. *All My Children* 9.1

1984-1985 Season

- 1. *General Hospital* 9.1
- 2. *All My Children* 8.2

1985-1986 Season (HH Ratings)

- 1. *General Hospital* 9.2
- 3. *All My Children* 8.0

1986-1987 Season

- 1. *General Hospital* 8.3
- 4. *All My Children* 7.0 (Tied with Days of our Lives and As the World Turns)

1987-1988 Season

- 1. *The Young and the Restless* 8.1 (Tied with General Hospital)
- 3. *All My Children* 7.7 (Tied with One Life to Live)

1988-1989 Season (HH Ratings)

- 1. *The Young and the Restless* 8.1
- 4. *All My Children* 6.7

1990s ratings

1989-1990 Season (HH Ratings) (1 = 921,000 Homes)

- 1. *The Young and the Restless* 8.0
- 3. *All My Children* 6.5

1990-1991 Season (HH Ratings)

- 1. *The Young and the Restless* 8.1
- 3. *All My Children* 6.2

1991-1992 Season (HH Ratings)

- 1. *The Young and the Restless* 8.2
- 2. *All My Children* 6.8

1992-1993 Season (HH Ratings)

- 1. *The Young and the Restless* 8.4
- 2. *All My Children* 7.3

1993-1994 Season (HH Ratings) (1 = 942,000 Homes)

- 1. *The Young and the Restless* 8.6
- 2. *All My Children* 6.6

1994-1995 Season (HH Ratings)

- 1. *The Young and the Restless* 7.5
- 2. *All My Children* 6.1

1995 Ratings (Millions of Viewers)

- 1. *The Young and the Restless* 7.155
- 2. *All My Children* 5.891
- 3. *General Hospital* 5.343
- 4. *The Bold and the Beautiful* 5.247
- 5. *One Life to Live* 5.152

1995-1996 Season (HH Ratings)

- 1. *The Young and the Restless* 7.7
- 4. *All My Children* 5.3

1996-1997 Season

- 1. *The Young and the Restless* 7.1
- 5. *All My Children* 4.7

1997-1998 Season

- 1. *The Young and the Restless* 7.0
- 5. *All My Children* 4.2

1998-1999 Season (HH Ratings)

- 1. *The Young and the Restless* 6.9
- 5. *All My Children* 3.9

2000s ratings

1999-2000 Season (HH Ratings) (Nielsen)

- 1. *The Young and the Restless* 6.8
- 5. *All My Children* 3.9

2000-2001 Season

- 1. *The Young and the Restless* 5.8
- 6. *All My Children* 3.4

2001-2002 Season

- 1. *The Young and the Restless* 5.0
- 6. *All My Children* 3.3

2002-2003 Season

- 1. *The Young and the Restless* 4.7
- 5. *All My Children* 3.0

2003-2004 Season

- 1. *The Young and the Restless* 4.4
- 4. *All My Children* 2.9

2004-2005 Season

- 1. *The Young and the Restless* 4.2
- 4. *All My Children* 2.9

2005-2006 Season (HH Ratings)

- 1. *The Young and the Restless* 4.2
- 4. *All My Children* 2.6

2006-2007 Season (HH Ratings)

- 1. *The Young and the Restless* 4.2
- 5. *All My Children* 2.3

2007-2008 Season (HH Ratings)

- 1."The Young and the Restless" 4.0
- 5. All My Children 2.2

2008-2009 Season

- 1. "The Young and the Restless" 3.7
- 5. All My Children 2.0

2010s ratings

2009-2010 Season

- 1. "The Young and the Restless" 3.7
- 5. All My Children 2.0

Record lows

The show reached a record low of 1,931,000 viewers on August 22, 2008. Its previous low was 2,144,000 viewers on November 2, 2007. (Nielsen Media Research)

Scheduling history

All My Children currently airs Monday through Friday at 1 p.m. eastern (12 p.m. central) on ABC. Encores are aired on SOAPnet in primetime at 8 p.m. (7 p.m.), late nights at 1 a.m. (12 a.m.), and early mornings at 7 a.m. (6 a.m.). The week's episodes air in a marathon on Sunday nights at 12 a.m. (11 p.m.).

From January 1970 to July 1975, the show aired for thirty minutes at 1 p.m. (12 p.m.), but when the new *Ryan's Hope* premiered, *All My Children* was bumped up a half-hour to 12:30 p.m. (11:30 a.m.). It returned to its original timeslot in January 1977 and has been there since, expanding to sixty minute episodes on April 25, 1977.

Schedule

- January 5, 1970 – July 4, 1975: 1:00–1:30 PM (12:00–12:30 PM, CT/PT)
- July 7, 1975 – January 14, 1977: 12:30–1:00 PM (11:30 AM–12:00 PM, CT/PT)
- January 17, 1977 – April 22, 1977: 1:00–1:30 PM (12:00–12:30 PM, CT/PT)
- April 25, 1977 – present: 1:00–2:00 PM (12:00–1:00 PM, CT/PT)

International broadcasting

In Australia, *All My Children* airs on free to air channel 7Two at 11am weekdays. 7Two are currently airing episodes from 2007.

In Italy, *All My Children*, under the title *La valle dei pini* (*Pine Valley*), started to air on Canale 5 in September 1985 at 2.30 P.M. , with episodes four years behind the U.S. In January 1987, it was moved to another channel, Rete 4, always at 2.30 P.M. . At the end of the decade, *La valle dei pini* began airing in late afternoon (and from September 1990 with only half U.S. episode each evening), after a bunch of Latin American telenovelas and before *General Hospital*. Then, in September 1991, the show was moved to 9.00 A.M. . *All My Children* was cancelled in May 1992, with episodes at that time six years behind the U.S..

All My Children is broadcast in South Africa every weekday at 3:00 pm CAT, after previously being aired at 10:30 am. Episodes are currently four years behind.

All My Children currently airs on A 12 PM PT,1 PM ET in Canada. AMC was also previously seen on Citytv stations in Calgary CKAL-TV, Edmonton CKEM-TV,and Winnipeg CHMI-TV. Prior to 1998, *All My Children* aired on the CBC Television network.

In Solomon Islands, AMC aired on Solomon Islands Broadcasting Corporation Mondays to Friday at 1:00pm.

Awards and nominations

Here is the list of the winners at the Daytime Emmy Awards; the show and its performers have been nominated in excess of 250 times.

Show

- 1981 "Outstanding Drama Series Writing Team"
- 1988 "Outstanding Drama Series Writing Team"
- 1992 "Outstanding Drama Series"
- 1994 "Outstanding Drama Series"
- 1995 "Outstanding Drama Series Directing Team"
- 1995 "Outstanding Technical Direction/Electronic Camera/Video Control"
- 1995 "Outstanding Live and Tape Sound Mixing and Sound Effects"
- 1996 "Outstanding Drama Series Writing Team"
- 1997 "Outstanding Drama Series Writing Team"
- 1998 "Outstanding Drama Series"
- 1998 "Outstanding Drama Series Writing Team"
- 1998 "Outstanding Makeup"
- 1998 "Outstanding Multiple Camera Editing"
- 1998 "Outstanding Live and Direct To Tape Sound Mixing"
- 1999 "Outstanding Music Direction And Composition"
- 2001 "Outstanding Achievement in Multiple Camera Editing"
- 2001 "Outstanding Achievement in Hairstyling"
- 2002 "Outstanding Achievement in Casting"
- 2002 "Outstanding Achievement in Costume Design"
- 2002 "Outstanding Achievement in Technical Direction/Electronic Camera/Video Control"
- 2002 "Outstanding Achievement in Music Direction and Composition"
- 2003 "Outstanding Drama Series Directing Team"
- 2005 "Outstanding Achievement in Music Direction and Composition for a Drama Series" (tied with *One Life to Live*)

- 2007 "Outstanding Achievement In Technical Direction/Electronic Camera/Video Control"
- 2008 "Outstanding Achievement in Technical Direction/ Electronic Camera/ Video Control"
- 2009 "Outstanding Art Direction/Set Decoration/Scenic Design"
- 2009 "Outstanding Lighting Direction"
- 2009 "Outstanding Live & Direct To Tape Sound Mixing"
- 2009 "Outstanding Technical Direction/Electronic Camera/Video Control" (tied with *The Young and the Restless*)
- 2010 "Outstanding Achievement in Costume Design"
- 2010 "Outstanding Lighting Direction"
- 2010 "Outstanding Makeup"

Individuals

- 1980 "Outstanding Supporting Actor in a Drama Series" Warren Burton (Eddie Dorrance)
- 1980 "Outstanding Supporting Actress in a Drama Series" Francesca James (Kitty Shea Davis/Kelly Cole Tyler)
- 1982 "Outstanding Supporting Actress in a Drama Series" Dorothy Lyman (Opal Cortlandt)
- 1983 "Outstanding Lead Actress in a Drama Series" Dorothy Lyman (Opal Cortlandt)
- 1983 "Outstanding Supporting Actor in a Drama Series" Darnell Williams (Jesse Hubbard)
- 1985 "Outstanding Lead Actor in a Drama Series" Darnell Williams (Jesse Hubbard)
- 1986 "Outstanding Lead Actor in a Drama Series" David Canary (Adam Chandler/Stuart Chandler)
- 1986 "Outstanding Younger Actor in a Drama Series" Michael E. Knight (Tad Martin)
- 1987 "Outstanding Supporting Actress in a Drama Series" Kathleen Noone (Ellen Shepherd)
- 1987 "Outstanding Younger Actor in a Drama Series" Michael E. Knight (Tad Martin)
- 1988 "Outstanding Lead Actor in a Drama Series" David Canary (Adam Chandler/Stuart Chandler)
- 1988 "Outstanding Supporting Actress in a Drama Series" Ellen Wheeler (Cindy Parker Chandler)
- 1989 "Outstanding Lead Actor in a Drama Series" David Canary (Adam Chandler/Stuart Chandler)
- 1989 "Outstanding Supporting Actress in a Drama Series" Debbi Morgan (Angie Baxter) (Tied with Nancy Lee Grahn for *Santa Barbara*)
- 1990 "Outstanding Supporting Actress in a Drama Series" Julia Barr (Brooke English)
- 1990 "Outstanding Younger Actress in a Drama Series" Cady McClain (Dixie Cooney Martin)
- 1993 "Outstanding Lead Actor in a Drama Series" David Canary (Adam Chandler/Stuart Chandler)
- 1995 "Outstanding Younger Actress in a Drama Series" Sarah Michelle Gellar (Kendall Hart)
- 1998 "Outstanding Supporting Actress in a Drama Series" Julia Barr (Brooke English)
- 1999 "Outstanding Lead Actress in a Drama Series" Susan Lucci (Erica Kane)
- 2001 "Outstanding Lead Actor in a Drama Series" David Canary (Adam Chandler/Stuart Chandler)
- 2001 "Outstanding Supporting Actor in a Drama Series" Michael E. Knight (Tad Martin)
- 2002 "Outstanding Supporting Actor in a Drama Series" Josh Duhamel (Leo du Pres)
- 2004 "Lifetime Achievement Award" Ray MacDonnell (Joe Martin)

- 2004 "Lifetime Achievement Award" Ruth Warrick (Phoebe Tyler Wallingford)
- 2005 "Outstanding Younger Actress in a Drama Series" Eden Riegel (Bianca Montgomery)
- 2009 "Outstanding Supporting Actor in a Drama Series" Vincent Irizarry (David Hayward) (Tied with Jeff Branson for *Guiding Light*.)
- 2010 "Lifetime Achievement Award" Agnes Nixon (Creator)

In 2010, *All My Children* was nominated for a GLAAD Media Award for "Outstanding Daily Drama" during the 21st GLAAD Media Awards.

Executive producers and head writers

Main article: List of All My Children crew

Executive producers

Duration	Name
January 5, 1970 to 1978	Agnes Nixon and Bud Kloss
1978 to 1982	Agnes Nixon and Jorn Winther
1982 to January 1986	Jacqueline Babbin [3]
January 1986 to March 1986	Jorn Winther
March 1986 to January 1989	Stephen Schenkel
January 1989 to April 1996	Felicia Minei Behr
April 1996 to April 1998	Francesca James
April 1998 to September 2003	Jean Dadario Burke
September 19, 2003 to October 24, 2003	Casey Childs
October 25, 2003 to present	Julie Hanan Carruthers

Head writers

Duration	Name
1970 to 1983	Agnes Nixon
1983 to 1986	Wisner Washam
1986 to 1987	Wisner Washam & Lorraine Broderick
1987 to 1989	Lorraine Broderick
January 1989 to March 1989	Lorraine Broderick & Victor Miller
March 1989 to December 1989	Margaret DePriest
December 1989 to May 1992	Agnes Nixon
May 1992 to April 1995	Megan McTavish
April 1995 to June 1995	Agnes Nixon (interim)
June 1995 to December 1997	Lorraine Broderick
December 1997 to February 1999	Megan McTavish
February 1999 to June 1999	Agnes Nixon
June 1999 to November 1999	Agnes Nixon, Elizabeth Page, and Jean Passanante
November 1999 to January 2001	Agnes Nixon and Jean Passanante
January 2001 to August 2001	Jean Passanante (with Michael Conforti in May, 2001)
August 2001-September 2001	No Head Writer credited
September 2001 to December 2002	Richard Culliton
December 2002 to March 2003	Gordon Rayfield
March 2003 to June 2003	Gordon Rayfield and Anna Cascio
July 2003 to February 2007	Megan McTavish
May 2007 to July 25, 2007	No Head Writer Credited
July 26, 2007 to January 14, 2008	James Harmon Brown and Barbara Esensten
January 15, 2008 to January 30, 2008	Julie Hanan Carruthers and Brian Frons (WGA strike)
January 31, 2008 to August 26, 2008	James Harmon Brown and Barbara Esensten
August 27, 2008 to November 20, 2009	Charles Pratt, Jr.
November 22, 2009 to March 12, 2010	Lorraine Broderick (interim)
March 15, 2010–Present	David Kreizman and Donna Swajeski

Directors

Jill Ackles, Larry Auerbach, James A. Baffico, Jack Coffey, Jean Dadario Burke, Christopher Goutman, Sherrell Hoffman, Del Hughes, Henry Kaplan, Andrew Lee, Robert Scinto, Susan Simon, Diana B. Wenman

Producers

Felicia Minei Behr, Jean Dadario Burke, Michael Laibson, Heidi Adam, Terry Cacavio, Thomas DeVilliers, Lisa Connor, Linda Laundra, Stephen Schenkel, Nancy Horwich

Writers

Neal Bell, Clarice Blackburn, Bettina F. Bradbury, Craig Carlson, Cathy Chicos, Hal Corley, Christina Covino, Carolyn Culliton, William Delligan, Judith Donato, Caroline Franz, Sharon Epstein, Charlotte Gibson, David Hiltrand, Janet Iacobuzio, Anita Jaffe, Frederick Johnson, Susan Kirshenbaum, Kathleen Klein, N. Gail Lawrence, Mimi Leahy, Kathleen Klein, Karen Lewis, Taylor Miller, Victor Miller, Jane Owen Murphy, Juliet Law Packer, Michelle Patrick, John PiRoman, Pete T. Rich, John Saffron, Courtney Simon, Peggy Sloan, Elizabeth Smith, Gillian Spencer, Millee Taggart, Ralph Wakefield, Elizabeth Wallace, Addie Walsh, Mary K. Wells, Jack Wood, Rodney Christopher, Laura Siggia, Moses Thomas Greene, Wisner Washam

Current crew

Writers	Producers/Consultants	Directors
Lorraine Broderick, Tara K. Walsh, Lisa Connor, Chip Hayes, Christopher Dunn, Kate Hall, Joanna Cohen, Rebecca Taylor, Jeff Beldner, Addie Walsh, James Harmon Brown, Barbara Esensten	Julie Hanan Carruthers (Executive Producer), Karen Johnson, Nadine Aronson, Barry Gingold, Joann Busiglio, Enza Dolce, Brian Frons	Casey Childs, Steven Williford, Conal O'Brien, Angela Tessinari, Barbara M. Simmons, Jill Ackles, Michael V. Pomarico, Francesca James, Shelley Curtis, Judy Blye Wilson

Merchandising

The game company TSR, Inc. introduced the *All My Children* game in 1985, based on the daytime drama. The game sold more than 150,000 copies.

DVD

A DVD was released on January 24, 2004 titled *Daytime's Greatest Weddings* which contained *All My Children* and other daytime soaps' weddings.

External links

- Official website [4]
- Watch "All My Children" Episodes Online [5]
- SOAPnet.com [6]

One Life to Live

One Life to Live	
Title card (2004—present)	
Alternate titles	*OLTL*
Genre	Soap opera
Creator(s)	Agnes Nixon
Senior cast member(s)	Erika Slezak Robert S. Woods Robin Strasser Hillary B. Smith Kassie DePaiva
Country of origin	United States
No. of episodes	10,790 (as of October 7, 2010)
Production	
Executive producer(s)	Frank Valentini
Head writer(s)	Ron Carlivati
Distributor	ABC
Running time	30 minutes (1968—1976) 45 minutes (1976—1978) 60 minutes (1978—present)
Broadcast	
Original channel	ABC
Original run	July 15, 1968 – present
External links	
Official website [1]	

One Life to Live (*OLTL*) is an American soap opera which, since July 15, 1968, has been broadcast on the ABC television network. Created by Agnes Nixon the series was the first daytime drama to primarily feature racially and socioeconomically diverse characters and consistently emphasize social issues.

Actress Erika Slezak has portrayed central heroine Victoria "Viki" Lord on *One Life to Live* since March 1971 and has won a record six Daytime Emmy Awards for the role. In 2002 the series won an Emmy for Outstanding Drama Series. Daily repeat broadcasts of the series appear weeknights on

SOAPnet with a day-behind repeat airing the following weekday morning and a rebroadcast of all the previous week's episodes on Saturday nights.

Creation

Impressed with the ratings success of NBC's *Another World*, ABC sought out *Another World* writer Nixon to create a serial for them. Though Nixon's concept for the new series was "built along the classic soap formula of a rich family and a poor family," she was "tired of the restraints imposed by the WASPy, noncontroversial nature of daytime drama." *One Life to Live* would emphasize "the ethnic and socioeconomic diversity" of the characters in its fictional setting. Nixon would go on to create *All My Children* in 1970 and *Loving* in 1983.

The initial main titles of the series featured the image of a roaring fireplace, a visual representation of the originally proposed title — *Between Heaven and Hell* — ultimately changed to *One Life to Live* to avoid controversy. *OLTL*'s first sponsors were the Colgate-Palmolive company, who also sponsored *The Doctors*. ABC bought the show from Nixon in December 1974 when they purchased all stock to her Creative Horizons Inc. The show was originally a half-hour serial until it was expanded to 45 minutes on July 23, 1976, and to one hour on January 16, 1978.

Series history

One Life to Live is set in the fictional city of Llanview, a suburb of Philadelphia, Pennsylvania. The show originally concentrated on the wealthy Lord family, the less wealthy Siegels (the first attempt to showcase a Jewish family on daytime television), the middle-class Rileys and Woleks, and the African-American Grays. *One Life to Live* has been called "the most peculiarly American of soap operas: the first serial to present a vast array of ethnic types, broad comic situations, a constant emphasis on social issues, and strong male characters."

Since its inception, *One Life to Live* has centered on the character of Victoria "Viki" Lord (originated by Gillian Spencer), who has been portrayed by six-time Emmy winner Erika Slezak since March 1971. Long-suffering heroine Viki has weathered love and loss, widowhood, rape, divorce, stroke and breast cancer, and has been memorably plagued by dissociative identity disorder (or DID, once known as multiple personality disorder) on and off for decades. Viki has also had heart problems, leading up to having the heart of her dying husband transplanted into her, to save her life.

The 1993 story of Marty Saybrooke's gang rape has been called "one of the show's most remembered and impactful."

One Life to Live celebrated its 40th anniversary in July 2008 with the return of several former cast members and by revisiting notable plotlines from its past. "Deceased" characters and even creator Agnes Nixon appeared in a storyline in which Slezak's Viki dies and visits Heaven, an homage to Viki's 1987 heavenly trip. Daytime Emmy-nominee Andrea Evans and others returned for a tribute to

Tina Lord's famous 1987 plunge over the Iguazu Falls and the 1990 royal wedding in fictional Mendorra. And like the 1988 Old West storyline in which the character Clint Buchanan steps back 100 years in the past, on July 21, 2008, Robert S. Woods began an extended storyline in which his character Bo Buchanan finds himself transplanted back into his own past—specifically 1968, the year of the series' inception—witnessing his family's back-story unfold. *Soap Opera Digest* subsequently named *One Life to Live* their "Best Show" of 2008, calling it "the year's most compelling" series and citing a myriad of storylines the magazine found "heartbreaking", "stunning", and "gripping", as well as complimenting its risk-taking and "diverse and talented" cast.

On August 4, 2009 it was announced that *One Life to Live*, which tapes in New York City, would move from ABC Studio 17 at 56 West 66th Street to Studio 23 at 320 West 66th Street Manhattan in early 2010. This studio was made available by the move of sister soap opera *All My Children* to a production facility in Los Angeles, where that series began taping on January 4, 2010. The new studio is 30% larger than *One Life to Live*'s previous one, and both *One Life to Live* and *All My Children* were to be taped and broadcast in high-definition (HD) after their moves. On October 8, 2009, ABC announced that it had postponed the transition to HD for *One Live to Live*, citing the economic climate at the time, though an ABC spokesperson did state that they "...will re-examine it next year." *One Life to Live* is the last remaining American daytime soap opera being produced in the New York City area.

Cast and characters

Main article: List of One Life to Live cast members

See also: List of One Life to Live characters

Controversy

In 2002, the popularity of antihero Todd Manning (Roger Howarth) prompted ABC to market a rag doll of the character, complete with his signature scar. First offered for sale on April 29, 2002, the doll was pulled on May 7, 2002 after a backlash begun when *The Jack Myers Report* "harshly criticized the network's judgment" on creating and releasing a doll based on Manning, a character who had notably been convicted of rape in 1993. *The New York Times* later quoted then-ABC President Angela Shapiro admitting, "I was insensitive and take total responsibility for it. I should have been sensitive to the history of the character and I wasn't."

Shortly after receiving a March 2005 GLAAD Media Award for its coverage of LGBT issues, *One Life to Live* was met with criticism when married district attorney Daniel Colson (Mark Dobies) was revealed to have murdered two people to cover up the fact that he is secretly gay. GLAAD itself criticized the storyline "for reinforcing the idea that being gay is something to be ashamed of," while *TV Guide* noted "It's hard to disagree with those who say that's a lousy representation of gay folks." Executive Producer Frank Valentini defended the story, saying "This is a story about the harsher side of intolerance and about one man not being true to himself. There are going to be meaningful, frank discussions that come out of this." Then-head writer Dena Higley explained, "The number one rule of soap opera is never cut drama. Daniel being gay and keeping that a secret is a dramatic story."

In June 2009, actress Patricia Mauceri (a performer on the series since 1995) was reportedly replaced in her role as Latin matriarch Carlotta Vega after voicing personal religious objections to a planned storyline in which Carlotta would be supportive of a gay relationship.

Historical storylines

- Storylines: 1968–1979
- Storylines: 1980–1989
- Storylines: 1990–1999
- Storylines: 2000–2010

Crossovers

Since the show's inception, the plotlines of *One Life to Live* have been established as existing in the same fictional universe as other ABC-owned daytime series, in particular Agnes Nixon's *All My Children*, which premiered in 1970. As noted from time to time in both series, fictional Pine Valley—the setting of *All My Children*—is located in Pennsylvania near *One Life to Live*'s Llanview. Over the years, many characters have crossed over from one series to another in both short appearances and extended runs. As early as 1968, *General Hospital*'s Dr. Steve Hardy appeared in Llanview to consult on Meredith Lord Wolek's blood disease as a means to lead *General Hospital* viewers to the new series; similarly, *One Life to Live*'s Dr. Larry Wolek visited *All My Children* shortly after its premiere in 1970.

In 1999, Daytime Emmy Award-winner Linda Dano returned to *One Life to Live* as Gretel "Rae" Cummings, a character she had previously played on the series from 1978 to 1980. In a 2000 move of network synergy designed to "entice viewers to tune into soap operas that they might not have usually watched," then-President of ABC Daytime Angela Shapiro orchestrated Dano's concurrent appearance as Rae on the three other ABC soap operas at the time — *All My Children*, *General Hospital*, and *Port Charles* — in an extended crossover storyline which was the first time a daytime character had ever appeared on four series. Rae's search for the child she had given up for adoption takes her to *All My Children*, where she discovers in 2000 that her own birth mother is Pine Valley's Myrtle Fargate. Following clues to *Port Charles* and *General Hospital*, Rae finally finds her daughter back in Llanview on *One Life to Live*: Skye Chandler, herself a former *All My Children* character who had relocated to *One Life to Live* in 1999. Skye's adopted *All My Children* father Adam Chandler appears on *One Life to Live* in 2001, and Rae initially identifies Skye's biological father as Alan Quartermaine of *General Hospital*. Both women subsequently appear on that series, with Skye moving to *General Hospital* full-time in 2001 and Rae returning to *One Life to Live* until 2004, making some appearances on *General Hospital* later in 2002 and 2003.

A December 30, 2003 visit by *One Life to Live*'s Paul Cramer to his estranged secret wife Babe Carey on *All My Children* ultimately leads to an extensive 2004 "baby switch" storyline which features crossovers of over 20 characters between the two series. With his sister Kelly desperate for a child to save her marriage after miscarrying her own, Paul finds himself delivering the babies of both Babe and her friend Bianca Montgomery during a rainstorm and subsequent flood in nearby Pine Valley on March 24, 2004. Paul stages a crash with his MEDEVAC helicopter; he takes Babe's son for Kelly, gives Bianca's daughter to Babe, and tells Bianca that her baby had died in the accident. Unaware of the child's origins, Kelly brings Babe's infant back to Llanview, passing him off as her child with her husband Kevin Buchanan. Months later, Babe discovers that her daughter is really the grieving Bianca's, but remains silent and allows Paul to manipulate her. Meanwhile, a devastated Kelly discovers that Paul had stolen her son from his mother and, desperate for cash, he blackmails Kelly by threatening to reveal the secret to Kevin. Bianca's daughter is returned to her for Christmas 2004, and once Kevin learns the truth, he and Kelly return Babe's son as well in 2005.

Awards

One Life to Live and many of its actors and crew have been nominated for dozens of awards, winning on many occasions. Erika Slezak has received six Daytime Emmy Awards for her acting, a feat tied only by Anthony Geary and Justin Deas.

In 2005 the series was awarded a GLAAD Media Award for its coverage of LGBT issues in the 2004 coming out storyline of gay character Mark Solomon (Matt Cavenaugh). *One Life to Live* was nominated again in 2010 for a well-publicized storyline in which police officer Oliver Fish comes out and reunites with his college boyfriend.

Daytime Emmy Award wins

Category	Recipient	Role	Year(s)
Outstanding Drama Series			2002
Lead Actor	Al Freeman, Jr. Robert S. Woods	Ed Hall Bo Buchanan	1979 1983
Lead Actress	Judith Light Robin Strasser Erika Slezak Hillary B. Smith Susan Haskell	Karen Wolek Dorian Lord Victoria Lord Nora Gannon Marty Saybrooke	1980, 1981 1982 1984, 1986, 1992, 1995, 1996, 2005 1994 2009
Supporting Actor	Thom Christopher	Carlo Hesser	1992

| Supporting Actress | Susan Haskell | Marty Saybrooke | 1994 |
| Younger Actor | Roger Howarth | Todd Manning | 1994 |

Wins in other categories

- 2009 Outstanding Achievement in Costume Design for a Drama Series
- 2009 Outstanding Achievement in Makeup for a Drama Series
- 2009 Outstanding Drama Series Directing Team
- 2009 Outstanding Original Song
- 2008 Outstanding Achievement in Costume Design for a Drama Series
- 2008 Outstanding Achievement in Lighting Direction for a Drama Series
- 2008 Outstanding Drama Series Directing Team
- 2008 Outstanding Drama Series Writing Team
- 2008 Outstanding Original Song (two awards for two *One Life to Live* songs, which tied)
- 2007 Outstanding Achievement in Art Direction/Set Decoration/Scenic Design for a Drama Series
- 2007 Outstanding Achievement in Multiple Camera Editing for a Drama Series
- 2005 Outstanding Achievement in Music Direction and Composition for a Drama Series (tied with *All My Children*)
- 2005 Outstanding Achievement in Technical Direction/Electronic Camera/Video Control for a Drama Series
- 2003 Outstanding Achievement in Live & Direct to Tape Sound Mixing for a Drama Series
- 2001 Outstanding Achievement in Live & Direct to Tape Sound Mixing for a Drama Series
- 2001 Outstanding Achievement in Technical Direction/Electronic Camera/Video Control for a Drama Series
- 2000 Outstanding Achievement in Costume Design for a Drama Series
- 2000 Outstanding Achievement in Live & Direct to Tape Sound Mixing for a Drama Series
- 2000 Outstanding Achievement in Music Direction and Composition for a Drama Series
- 2000 Outstanding Original Song
- 1994 Outstanding Drama Series Writing Team
- 1987 Outstanding Drama Series Writing Team
- 1984 Outstanding Achievement in Technical Excellence for a Daytime Drama Series
- 1984 Outstanding Direction for a Daytime Drama Series
- 1983 Outstanding Direction for a Daytime Drama Series
- 1982 Outstanding Achievement in Any Area of Creative Technical Crafts: Lighting Direction (Everett Melosh)
- 1976 Outstanding Individual Director for a Daytime Drama Series (David Pressman)
- 1974 Outstanding Technical Direction and Electronic Camerawork

Scheduling/ratings history

For historical ratings information, see List of US daytime soap opera ratings

ABC cemented its reputation as a youth-oriented network in daytime with the addition of *OLTL* to its schedule, with much of the rest of its lineup consisting of fashionable soaps like *Dark Shadows,* sitcom reruns, and game shows packaged by Chuck Barris. The network placed the new serial at 3:30 p.m./2:30 Central, against CBS' established hit *Edge of Night* and the popular NBC game *You Don't Say. OLTL* replaced the short-lived *Baby Game,* in a three-way shuffle with *Dark Shadows* and *Dating Game.*

Despite the tough competition, the intense tone of the plot and strong characters allowed the show to get a leg up on *YDS,* wearing that game down to the point of its cancellation in September 1969; NBC replaced the Tom Kennedy-hosted game in that timeslot with three unsuccessful serials: *Bright Promise* (1969–1972), *Return to Peyton Place* (1972–1974), and *How to Survive a Marriage* (1974–1975).

Things greatly improved for *OLTL* in 1972, when CBS relocated *Edge* in response to packager Procter and Gamble's demands. The four-year-old show managed to top the ratings for the first time over CBS' declining *Secret Storm,* and later, the game *Hollywood's Talking,* which ran only 13 weeks. However, trouble loomed on the horizon as *OLTL* anticipated its fifth birthday, with the coming of CBS' revival of Goodson-Todman's *Match Game.* Some months after its debut in July 1973, that show became the daytime phenomenon of the mid-1970s, becoming the top-rated of all daytime shows by Thanksgiving. ABC stood by *OLTL,* however, keeping it put at 3:30/2:30.

By 1975, though, NBC became a serious player in that timeslot for the first time in over five years when it expanded its strong soap *Another World* to a full hour, its second half occupying the 3:30/2:30 period. This would cause *OLTL* to lose a substantial audience share, but its lead-in, *General Hospital,* experienced even worse losses. ABC decided to take an unusual approach in addressing the competition: it expanded both *OLTL* and *GH* to 45 minutes, with each composing a half of a 90-minute block between 2:30/1:30 and 4/3. Beginning on July 26, 1976, *OLTL* assumed the first position, at 2:30/1:30. ABC bet its hopes on viewers staying tuned past the half hour, making them unlikely to switch channels to *AW* or *All in the Family* reruns on CBS (for *GH* fans, turning to *Match Game*).

This approach showed some promise, until November 7, 1977, when CBS expanded *Guiding Light* to a full hour at 2:30/1:30. As *OLTL* struggled, its neighbor, *GH,* was in danger of cancellation after a 15-year run. So, in a "make it or break it" ultimatum to *GH,* ABC finally gave an hour to both shows, on January 16, 1978, with *OLTL* occupying the 2-3/1-2 p.m. slot; *The $20,000 Pyramid,* which enjoyed three solid years of success at 2/1, got dispatched to Noon/11 a.m. for the rest of its ABC run, to make room for *OLTL.*

This proved to be decisive for the long-term survival of both shows, as *GH* rose rapidly to the top spot in the Nielsens through its brash, youthful storylines (culminating in the hugely popular "Luke and

Laura" storyline by 1979-1980). As for *OLTL,* from its tenth birthday onward, it took advantage of the decline in quality and popularity of its competitors, all Procter and Gamble productions. *Search for Tomorrow,* for instance, spent its last several months on CBS against the last half of *OLTL.* Its replacement, *Capitol,* which ran from 1982 to 1987, did little better, and after its cancellation, CBS aligned *As the World Turns* against *OLTL* and *AW,* a configuration that stayed in place until *AW's* cancellation in 1999. During the 2000s thus far, *OLTL* has run about even with *ATWT,* with NBC's *AW* replacement *Passions* trailing significantly (*Passions* was canceled by NBC in September 2007 and moved to the DirecTV channel The 101; the network no longer programs in that time slot).

One Life to Live enjoyed fair-to-middling ratings throughout most of its first decade, but rose rapidly as it entered its second, along with the rest of ABC's daytime lineup. The 1980s saw the show reach the height of its popularity, occupying a top-four place for almost all of the decade. Since 1991, it returned to the middle of the pack, but its numbers declined, in common with all other soaps. By decade's end, the show rested near the bottom of the ratings pack, and continues to hover around the lower reaches of the weekly ratings today, at least in terms of total number of viewers; however, the show does tend to rank in the mid-range for the target demographic of women aged 18-49, often higher than sister show *All My Children.*

Executive producers and head writers

Executive producers

Duration	Name
January 2003 to present	Frank Valentini
January 2001 to December 2002	Gary Tomlin
December 1997 to January 2001	Jill Farren Phelps
October 1996 to December 1997	Maxine Levinson
July 1994 to October 1996	Susan Bedsow Horgan
July 1991 to June 1994	Linda Gottlieb
August 1984 to June 1991	Paul Rauch
August 1983 to July 1984	Jean Arley
July 1977 to August 1983	Joseph Stuart
July 1968 to July 1977	Doris Quinlan

Head writers

Duration	Name(s)
May 2, 2008 to present	Ron Carlivati
February 15, 2008 to May 1, 2008	Gary Tomlin (During WGA strike)
September 11, 2007 to February 14, 2008	Ron Carlivati
May 8, 2007 to September 10, 2007	Dena Higley Ron Carlivati
December 13, 2004 to May 7, 2007	Dena Higley
November 29, 2004 to December 10, 2004	Brian Frons Frank Valentini
March 23, 2004 to November 24, 2004	Michael Malone
March 10, 2003 to March 22, 2004	Josh Griffith Michael Malone
February 3, 2003 to March 7, 2003	Josh Griffith
January 2001 to January 31, 2003	Lorraine Broderick Christopher Whitesell
September 1999 to March 2001	Megan McTavish
January 1999 to September 1999	No Headwriter was credited at this time
March 30th, 1998 to December 31, 1998	Pamela K. Long
June 1997 to March 29th 1998	Claire Labine Matthew Labine
December 1996-June 1997	Jean Passanante Peggy Sloane (co-headwriter)
April 1996 to December 1996	Leah Laiman Jean Passanante Peggy Sloane
March 1995 to March 1996	Michael Malone
January 1992 to February 1995	Josh Griffith Michael Malone
August 1991 to January 1992	Michael Malone
May 1991 to August 1991	Craig Carlson
September 1990 to May 1991	Craig Carlson and Leah Laiman
July 1987 to July 1990	S. Michael Schnessel
July 1984 to June 1987	Peggy O'Shea

December 1983 to June 1984	Sam Hall Peggy O'Shea
June 1983 to December 1983	John William Corrington Joyce Corrington
February 1983 to June 1983	Henry Slesar
July 1982 to January 1983	Sam Hall Henry Slesar
March 1980 to May 1982	Sam Hall Peggy O'Shea
November 1978 to March 1980	Gordon Russell Sam Hall
September 1973 to October 1978	Gordon Russell
August 1972 to September 1973	Agnes Nixon Gordon Russell
July 1968 to July 1972	Agnes Nixon Paul Roberts Don Wallace

International broadcasting

One Life to Live currently airs on Sun TV at 2:00 PM ET in Canada. Also airs on Joytv in Vancouver and Winnipeg Market at 1PM. The series was previously broadcast on A and the Citytv stations in Calgary (CKAL-TV), Edmonton (CKEM-TV), and Winnipeg (CHMI-TV). *One Life to Live* aired in the early 1990s on the CBC Television network following *All My Children*, but it was discontinued in 1997.

In Italy *One Life to Live*, under the title *Una vita da vivere*, aired in the afternoon from November 1982 to September 1985 on Canale 5 (1978-1981 US episodes). The series returned with new episodes in July 1988, this time on Rete 4 in the afternoon. In September 1989 it was moved to 8.30 am, and stopped airing in June 1991 (1984 UU episodes). Reruns aired from 1987 to 1990 on Italia 7 and briefly in 1994 on Tivù Italia.

130 episodes of *One Life to Live* from 1980-1981 were broadcast under the title *Solo se vive una vez* on Spain's TVE1 at 11.30 am starting on August 11, 1986.

In Israel *One Life to Live* debuted in 1994 on Channel 3 weekdays at 18:00 with the Marty Saybrooke gang rape storyline (US: 1993). It went off the air in 1998. In Summer 1999 the series was relaunched in prime time on the telenovela channel Viva (21:00), starting where the previous run of episodes had left off (US 1997 episodes). In 2001 *One Life to Live* was relocated again, this time to Yes Channel 3 satellite. It went off the air in May 2002 (2001 US episodes). In Israel, the show was named "את החיים

"לחיות" (Likhiot Et Hakhayim) - meaning "Living The Life".

See also

- List of longest-serving soap opera actors
- List of *One Life to Live* characters

External links

- Official website [1]
- *One Life to Live*: SOAPnet.com [2]
- *One Life to Live*: Soaps.com [3]
- *One Life to Live* [4] at the Internet Movie Database
- Llanview Labyrinth [5]

General Hospital

General Hospital	
General Hospital intertitle (February 23, 2010–present)	
Alternate titles	GH
Genre	Soap opera
Creator(s)	Frank and Doris Hursley
Senior cast member(s)	Leslie Charleson Anthony Geary Jane Elliot Kimberly McCullough John J. York John Ingle Jacklyn Zeman Rachel Ames Denise Alexander Steve Burton Maurice Bernard Vanessa Marcil
Country of origin	United States
Language(s)	English
No. of episodes	12,162 (as of October 13, 2010)
Production	
Executive producer(s)	Selig J. Seligman (1963) James Young (1963-1975) Tom Donovan (1975-1977) Gloria Monty (1978–1987, 1990–1992) H. Wesley Kenney (1987-1989) Joseph Hardy (1989-1990) Wendy Riche (1992–2001) Jill Farren Phelps (2001–present)
Running time	15 minutes (1963-1964) 30 minutes (1964–1976) 45 minutes (1976–1978) 60 minutes (1978–present)
Broadcast	
Original channel	ABC

Original run	April 1, 1963 – present
External links	
Official website [1]	

General Hospital (commonly abbreviated *GH*) is an American daytime television drama that is credited by the *Guinness Book of World Records* as the longest-running American soap opera currently in production and the third longest running drama in television in American history after *Guiding Light* and *As the World Turns*. It premiered on the ABC television network on April 1, 1963. Broadcast weekdays and currently repeated nightly on SOAPnet, it is the longest-running serial produced in Hollywood, and the longest-running entertainment program in ABC television history. *General Hospital* rose to the top of the ratings in the early 1980s in part thanks to the monumentally popular "supercouple" Luke and Laura, whose 1981 wedding brought in 30 million viewers and remains the highest-rated hour in American soap opera history. In 2003, *TV Guide* named *General Hospital* the 'Great Soap Opera of All Time.' In 2007, *General Hospital* was listed as one of *Time* magazine's "100 Best TV Shows of All-*TIME*." *General Hospital* became the longest running American soap opera in production when *As the World Turns* ended its run on September 17, 2010.

General Hospital was created by husband-and-wife soap writers Frank and Doris Hursley, and is set in the fictional city of Port Charles, New York. It was only the second soap to air on ABC (after the short-lived *Road to Reality*, which aired for several months during the 1960-61 season). Currently taped at The Prospect Studios, *General Hospital* originally aired for a half-hour. The series was expanded from 30 minutes to 45 minutes on July 23, 1976, and then to a full hour on January 16, 1978. It holds the record for most Daytime Emmy Awards for Outstanding Drama Series, with 10 wins. In 1964, a sister soap was created for *General Hospital*, *The Young Marrieds*. It ran for only two years, and was cancelled due to low ratings in 1966. *General Hospital* also spawned a prime time spin-off with the same name in the United Kingdom from 1972 to 1979, as well as the daytime series *Port Charles* (1997–2003) and the prime time spin-off *General Hospital: Night Shift* (2007–2008) in the United States.

In April 2009, CBS announced that it did not renew *Guiding Light*, which was canceled airing its final episode on September 18, 2009, which meant *General Hospital* became the second longest running American soap opera currently on air, after *As the World Turns*. On December 8, 2009, CBS announced that they were cancelling *As the World Turns* and its final episode aired on September 17, 2010. *General Hospital* then became the longest-running daytime soap opera still featured on American television, having aired continuously since April 1, 1963, and the British soap opera *Coronation Street* became world's longest-lived soap opera currently airing on television, having been on air since 1960.

With the cancellation of *Days of our Lives* airing its final episode on September 16, 2011, *General Hospital* will still be the longest-running soap opera on the air after 48 years, and *One Life to Live* will then become the second longest-running soap opera in production.

Show history

Main article: History of General Hospital

Launched in 1963, the first stories were mainly set at General Hospital in an unnamed mid-sized Eastern city (the name of the city, Port Charles, would not be mentioned until the 1970s), revolving around Dr. Steve Hardy (John Beradino) and his friend, Nurse Jessie Brewer (Emily McLaughlin). Steve was Chief of Internal Medicine on the hospital's seventh floor and dedicated his life to healing and caring for the sick, ably assisted by Nurse Jessie. Jessie's turbulent marriage to the much-younger Dr. Phil Brewer (originally portrayed by Roy Thinnes; lastly by Martin West) was the center of many early storylines. In 1964 the woman who would finally win Steve's heart, Audrey March, a former flight attendant came to town. Audrey's older sister, Lucille Weeks was a nurse at General Hospital. Lucille married hospital janitor, Al Weeks. Audrey married Dr. Tom Baldwin and had his son (played as an infant by the daughter of Audrey's portrayer Rachel Ames.) In 1973 Audrey married alcoholic Dr. Jim Hobart before finally realizing she loved Steve.

Other nurses that had an impact at General Hospital during the 60's and 70's included Meg Bentley. Meg was the mother to her young son Scotty and step-mother to troubled-teen Brooke Clinton. Meg married attorney Lee Baldwin, Tom Baldwin's brother. Lee adopted Scotty. When Meg died Lee became Scotty's only family. Several years later Lee met and married Caroline Chandler. Caroline died within a few years then Lee married Gail.

Diana Taylor was a young nurse torn between two men, Dr. Peter Taylor and Dr. Phil Brewer. Bouncy Sharon McGillis married shy Dr. Henry Pinkham. Jane Harland was married to businessman Howie Dawson. They had a daughter. Howie's mother, Mrs. Dawson, lived with them. At one point in about 1972, Howie soon became involved with Brooke Clinton.

Augusta McLeod came to General Hospital in 1973 and set in motion events that would impact General Hospital for years to come. It was Augusta that brought Phil Brewer back to GH to break up Peter and Diana Taylor. Augusta was pregnant with Peter's child. December 6, 1974, Phil Brewer was murdered by a geode (paper weight). Jessie Brewer was on trial for her life after having been caught with the deceased Phil holding the murder weapon. She was acquitted. Augusta McLeod was sent to prison for murder. She gave birth to her son which was given up for adoption.

The November 18, 1981 wedding of Luke and Laura, played by Anthony Geary and Genie Francis, was the most watched event in daytime serial history.

During the 1980s the series featured several high-profile action, adventure, and some science fiction based story lines. Location shooting at sites including Mt. Rushmore in South Dakota; Niagara Falls; Grand Ole Opry in Nashville, Tennessee; Atlantic City, New Jersey; Big Bear and Avalon (Catalina Island), California; and San Antonio, Texas are just some that propelled the story.

In the 1990s, *General Hospital* entered a transitional phase as the action/adventure storylines of the 1980s became less popular. The show gained critical acclaim for its sensitive handling of social issues, most notable of which were the heart transplant storyline which involved the death of eight-year-old BJ Jones (daughter of Dr. Tony Jones and R.N. Bobbie Spencer) in a bus crash and the subsequent donation of her heart to her dying cousin Maxie Jones. Shortly afterwards, Monica Quartermaine (Leslie Charleson) began a long battle with breast cancer, which led to her adopting Emily Quartermaine, a young girl who had been orphaned when her mother died of breast cancer. Her adopted daughter was later murdered by an unknown killer, leaving Dr. Monica Quartermanine heartbroken. GH was also praised for yet another storyline in the form of the beautiful but tragic love story of teenagers Stone Cates (Michael Sutton) and Robin Scorpio (Kimberly McCullough). After a struggle that lasted throughout most of 1995, Stone died from AIDS at the age of 19 and his death was followed by storylines in which 17 year old Robin had to deal with being HIV-positive as a result of her and Stone's relationship. The storyline got Sutton a Daytime Emmy nomination for Outstanding Supporting Actor and won McCullough an Outstanding Younger Actress award. ABC featured an "Afterschool Special" revolving around the AIDS story.

On Saturday, December 14, 1996, General Hospital aired its one of three primetime episodes, *General Hospital: Twist of Fate*, which picked up where that Friday's episode had left off. The special centered around Laura's supposed death at the hands of Stefan Cassadine.

The series' 11,000th episode aired on February 20, 2006.

On April 23, 2009, *General Hospital* became ABC's first regular daytime drama to be taped and broadcast in high definition, though the 2008 season of its primetime spin-off *General Hospital: Night Shift* was in high definition. This is the second daytime drama to move to high definition after CBS's *The Young and the Restless*.

On February 23, 2010, the series aired its 12,000th episode.

Production summary

Production summary

Start date	End date	Time slot(eastern)	Run time(minutes)	Network	Filming location	Notes
April 1, 1963	December 27, 1963	1:00 pm	30	ABC Television	Hollywood, California	—
December 30, 1963	July 23, 1976	3:00 pm				—
July 26, 1976	January 13, 1978	3:15 pm	45			—
January 16, 1978	Present	3:00 pm	60			—

Cast

See also: List of General Hospital cast members, List of General Hospital characters, Children of General Hospital, and List of General Hospital miscellaneous characters

Title sequence

Since the series' debut in 1963, *General Hospital* has had six opening title sequence packages and five theme songs.

From 1963 to 1967, the ABC announcer said "GENERAL HOSPITAL...brought to you by [product name]"; when the show moved to color on October 30, 1967, until circa early 1970s, announcer Ed Chandler would say, "GENERAL HOSPITAL in color". During the end of each scene just seconds before commercial break, Chandler would say "We'll return to GENERAL HOSPITAL in just a moment"; that announcement was phased out in the early 1970s. During 1973 to 1976, Chandler would simply say "*General Hospital*". "General Hospital" was the last ABC show to move to color.

For the closing credits sequence, Chandler's original line from late 1963-circa 1970s was, "This is Ed Chandler inviting you to tune in tomorrow (Monday) and every weekday for GENERAL HOSPITAL". It was changed during circa 1973 to "This is Ed Chandler inviting you to tune in every day, Monday through Friday for GENERAL HOSPITAL." This spiel was used until July 1976. Since 1976, the only show announcements are the daily sponsor tags by ABC staff announcers ("ABC's *General Hospital*, brought to you by..."), and until the late 1990s, that immediately preceded the title at the end of the opening sequence. Currently, these announcements are done on network bumpers after the first scene.

Although Ed Chandler ceased his live announcing duties for the show in July 1976, a recording of his voice was retained for the first mid-program bumper ("*General Hospital* will continue in a moment"). There continued to be two mid-bumpers until January 1978, when a third was added during mid-break, after station identification, representing the expansion to an hour. The latter two bumpers would have no announcement. The three-bumper format was in place until circa 1986, with only the first and last mid-bumpers remaining. Starting in 1986, a muted display of the zooming title from the opening sequence was inserted to accommodate the mandate for affiliates to run their station ID over a program's still or logo. Ed Chandler's recorded mid-break announcement on the first bumper lasted until 1989. From 1989 to 1992, the rotating staff of ABC announcers would say "*General Hospital* will continue in a moment"; well-known voice actor Bill Ratner was also commonly heard during this time. Then from the fall of 1992 until late-1999, various *GH* cast members would voice the first mid-bumper ("*General Hospital* will continue in a moment", with "here on ABC" being added to the line in 1996). Also, from late 1996 to September 1999, various cast members (but most often Ingo Rademacher (Jasper Jacks) would introduce next-episode previews off camera. Since the fall of 1999, mid-bumpers and previews have been done on network graphics. In 2008, due to tight budgets, ABC cut the spoiler promos.

April 1, 1963 - November 21, 1963	[2] In the early episodes of 1963, *General Hospital* used a scene of doctors and nurses going about their business in the hospital, which then freezes and turns into a negative image, with the title appearing in the Craw Clarendon Condensed font (which remained the same until 1993). Accompanying this was a delightful, rather expansive piano piece by Kip Walton. Mid-bumpers and closing sequences from day one featured the show's title, in the same font and size, centered on the screen against a black background. In the closings, a second sponsor plug would be included after the title, which would then return to the black screen where the credits would start running. In the first several years, credits would be carded one at a time for the most part on Monday-Thursday episodes; after production principals, the top billing stars would be credited (during this era, they were mainly John Beradino, Emily McLaughlin, Rachel Ames, Peter Hansen and Patricia Breslin). On Fridays, the entire credit setup would scroll, with full cast and crew. The top-billing stars would still appear in their stacked format during the scroll, as they did on carded days (with actors' name, "as" and their characters' name all on separate lines) while supporting players would appear with their characters' name positioned to the left followed by periods, with the actors' names listed below in capitals over on the right. All crew credits would be centered. The final display of the *General Hospital* title in all broadcasts would scroll up itself to include the Selmur Productions ident at the end of the sequence. The last episode to use this title, on November 22, 1963, was likely pre-empted by ABC as the news of assassination and death of President John F. Kennedy was unfolding during the afternoon.
November 26, 1963 - April 11, 1975 [2]	Nearly eight months into *General Hospital*'s run, the nurses' station opening sequence was changed in favor of a more simple display. At the end of the prologue, the first few notes of the opening theme began playing as the scene dissolved into a black screen, with the show's title appearing on it, centered. The same visual would remain on the screen for the length of the brief opening theme tune, save for a cut-in to a sponsor plug, and virtually only as long as the network announcer's (later Ed Chandler's) spiel. This second theme package was basically an expansion of the visual format used in the mid-bumpers and closing since the show's premiere. When the program moved to color in late October 1967, the black background used for all the visuals changed to blue, but otherwise the package would go unchanged for its entire run. The arrival of this first long-running setup for *GH* brought a revised version of the April-November 1963 theme, in a higher pitch and faster melody, which was also composed by Kip Walton. The same mid-bumpers and closing credits format from the first package remained in place. The Selmur Productions ident continued to appear at the conclusion of the credits every episode until 1968, when ABC bought complete ownership of *General Hospital*.

| April 14, 1975
- March 31,
1993 | The exterior shot of the hospital in the opening and ending credits is the General Hospital of the Los Angeles County-USC Medical Center, located just east of Downtown Los Angeles (Google Street View image from outside the gate:). This shot was used from 1975 to 1993, and remained relatively unchanged between those years. It consisted of an ambulance rushing through the gates of the medical center, followed by the show's title zooming outward from the view of the hospital. The sequence's theme song was led prominently by George Wright's piano theme from no later than Monday, April 14, 1975 until Friday, July 23, 1976. Then on Monday, July 26, 1976, the theme music was changed to "Autumn Breeze" by Jack Urbont, with the horns throughout the opening sequence (the 1975 opening sequence would remain the same). The graphic details of the opening would see only one alteration, in 1978, when the lettering of the show's zooming title became smaller. It is one of the longest running soap opera theme/visuals in history, with only the 1970-1989 theme/visuals of *All My Children* and *Days of our Lives*' 1972-93 package ahead of it. The sequence was used until the last episode of *General Hospital* with the Autumn Breeze theme aired on March 31, 1993. |

The closing credits during this long era were done over nearly the same exterior of the LA County-USC Medical Center, with the main difference here being a blue-sky/cloud visual, as opposed to the opening having a clear, sunny sky. Occasionally a closer pan of the hospital was used, but it became more common in the early 1980s and was used almost exclusively from 1983 until 1993. The Craw Clarendon Condensed credits continued the tradition of carding dayplayers one at a time on most days, with the actors' name on top, the "as" on the middle line and character name below. On Fridays or during special storylines, a long crawl credits format also remained. No earlier than the start of the LA-USC Medical Center visuals era, scrolling cast credits became reformatted where the actors name appeared first in capitals, positioned to the left and followed by periods, with their character's name seen below in mostly lowercase, set on the right. Copyright notice first appeared at the end of all episodes in 1980, in a small capitalized font. By late 1981, the notice began appearing in capitalized Arial font, and would remain this way through the fall of 1982.

In the fall of 1982, the closing format was updated so that now the credits were electronically generated. The creators' credit, which had long consisted of "Frank and" on one line, and "Doris Hursley" below it, now became "Frank &" with "Doris Hursley" underneath. The end credits became smaller, and the carded dayplayer setup now used the long-crawl formatting with the actors' name followed by periods, with character name below. From this point on, the more inward shot of the hospital was used full time. The copyright notice, which currently consisted of "(c) (year) American Broadcasting Companies, Inc.", was changed to small, capitalized Craw Clarendon Condensed, on two lines. Around the episode marking *GH*'s 20th anniversary in April 1983, "All Rights Reserved" was added below the copyright notice, in small, capitalized Arial. Between December 1983 and February 1984, the space between *General* and *Hospital* in the closing title displays was removed, so that the title was stacked together; and, "Frank & Doris Hurley" became "Frank And Doris" on one line, with "Hursley" below. At the beginning of 1985, Gloria Monty finally became credited as "Executive Producer", replacing the simple "Produced By" title which had been a standard from the early days of TV.

By 1988, the carded credits format had long become occasional, and ceased during that year. Thereafter, on days that had short closings, the credits scrolled production principals only up until the role of associate producer, which would then be followed by the closing title display and copyright. Beginning in September 1989, on long crawl days listing the cast, John Beradino and Emily McLaughlin's credits scrolled on screen one at a time before the rest of the cast was listed in the large group. This was a nod by then-executive producer H. Wesley Kenney to Beradino and McLaughlin's seniority to the program. When Emily McLaughlin died in 1991, Beradino was listed alone before the rest of the cast, with Rachel Ames now always leading first on the main cast list.

April 1, 1993 - August 27, 2004	Wendy Riche made her most visible change as she decided to retire the long-running 1976 opening in favor of something new. The new opening, "Faces Of The Heart" by Dave Koz, debuted at the beginning of the first episode on April 1, 1993 that marked General Hospital's thirtieth anniversary. The theme begins with a heartbeat rhythm played on a bass guitar as we dissolve to a shot of an ambulance. That, in turn, dissolves into a tinted, letterboxed view of the exterior of the LA County-USC Medical Center in Los Angeles, California. This is followed by a series of video headshots of all the contract cast members, either solo or in pairs, against a red background. After every few clips, there is an action clip from the show. At the end of the sequence, we go back to the letterboxed, tinted hospital exterior and the title of the show in Goudy Bold type. For the 32nd Anniversary week in April 1995, the theme was remixed with a longer version with a reprise at the end, also the cast montage had a major update, which several cast members received new footage and new Puerto Rico action scenes were added. On April 1, 2003, the show's 40th anniversary, the characters' first names were added to the opening.

For several weeks into the new "Faces of the Heart" package, the end credits remained in the same Craw Clarendon Condensed type used in past years. Now, however, the long crawl was done over stills from that day's episode. In one of the last episodes to use the Craw Clarendon Condensed, the closing credits were actually turned red, experimentally, to represent the color of the show's new visual image. By no later than early May 1993, the credits resumed being white and were now in Goudy font, to match the new *General Hospital* title logo. Short credit sequences either ran over episode stills or a variation of the red-tinted view of the hospital seen in the opening. This exterior background had motion effects that slowly pulled outward from the LA-USC building. From March 1996 to September 1999, each end credit segment was done in smaller lettering on a separate card for each still. The separate card setup is still used in the end titles shown on SoapNet rebroadcasts, but the credits are done over a shot of the hospital.

August 30, 2004 - February 22, 2010	During the May 2004 sweeps, ABC Daytime began a significant re-branding process. New graphics and new promotional bumpers were created, and the visuals in the new promos were incorporated into new openings that were unveiled on all three ABC soaps in subsequent weeks. On August 30, 2004, GH unveiled a new opening that incorporated many of the character visuals used in a new set of ABC Daytime promos and bumpers that debuted in May 2004. The nods to the show's past seem quite minimal in this new opening as we get only an extremely brief glimpse of an ambulance and an almost equally brief upward pan of the hospital exterior. This new opening sequence ends with a shot of the male cast members clad in tuxedos and posing against a white background, with Anthony Geary walking out of the shot, followed by the title of the show. The portion featuring the male cast members remained the same throughout this version's use, in spite of the fact that most of the cast members featured there such as Ted King, M'fundo Morrison, and Scott Clifton had left the show by the time it was retired. Though departing actors continued to be removed from the main part of the sequence as needed, no new actors were added from July 2007 until the version's retirement in February 2010. Contract actors such as Claire Coffee, Sarah Brown, Natalia Livingston (who was previously featured in the opening as Emily and later returned as Rebecca) and Nazanin Boniadi came and went without ever appearing in this opening. The title appears in white letters in a single line across the screen against a black background, which is framed by letterboxing. On April 20, 2009, this sequence was updated slightly - the open was stretched (and later cropped) to fill the 16x9 picture ratio for the show's move to HD, but the video quality of the opening was still in standard definition. It is during this era that main technical credits (including the day's producer, director, etc. and the Hursleys' creative credit (even though they had passed away years previously) began to appear during the opening prologue scene, a practice only two other soaps (*The Young and the Restless*, which are split between the prologue and first act in their case, and *All My Children*) currently utilize; *One Life to Live*'s technical credits appear after their opening credits.
February 23, 2010–present	On February 23, 2010, *General Hospital* debuted its revamped, HD opening credits in honor of the series' 12,000th episode. It features brand new shots of the cast members (shot in September 2009) and features debut opening sequence shots for cast members that have joined since fall 2007 (the last time the "Sirens" opening added characters), including (in order of initiation to contract cast) Sonya Eddy, Brandon Barash, Jason Cook, Nathan Parsons, Drew Garrett, Dominic Zamprogna, Lexi Ainsworth, and Lisa LoCicero, as well as the re-introduction of Jonathan Jackson. The opening was updated in April 2010 with the recasting of Michael Corinthos III, now played by Chad Duell, proving the new opening will be prompt with updates. The opening starts out with the word "General" going left, then giving a shot of virtual Port Charles. Next there is a picture of a siren and then the cast are shown as in its former style. With each character, the actor and character names are displayed, with character-themed background footage (such as Spoon Island behind Nikolas and the Haunted Star casino behind Luke). Following the character shots, Anthony Geary is seen turning away from the camera, as in the previous opening package. The credits end with the show logo, now in Goudy Old Style font, backgrounded by another skyline shot. The theme music from the previous sequence was carried over into this sequence.

With this sequence, the contract cast members' names began to appear during the opening credits, a practice only two other soaps (*The Young and the Restless*, though that show does not list all contract cast members, and *The Bold and the Beautiful*) currently utilize; all other soaps list their cast's names in the closing credits for one episode each week. The opening also utilizes character names as well, something only one other soap (*The Bold and the Beautiful*) does.

On May 24, 2010, a second opening debuted featuring Brianna Brown and Scott Reeves in place of Sonya Eddy and Jason Cook. Initially, rumors were rampant that the latter two had been released from their contracts but it was later shown that, for the first time, *General Hospital* was utilizing more than one opening in order to compensate for their sprawling cast. This remains the case as of August 11, 2010, when "General Hospital" continued to utilize more than one opening and added Vanessa Marcil Giovinazzo, who had returned to the show, to the sequence. One version of the opening includes Brianna Brown, Scott Reeves, and Leslie Charleson while the other has Sonya Eddy, Jason Cook, and John Ingle.

Main crew members

Main article: List of General Hospital crew

- **Producers:** Jill Farren Phelps (Executive Producer), Mary O'Leary, Mercer Barrows, Michelle Henry, Deborah Genovese, Robert Guza, Jr. (Consulting Producer)
- **Directors:** Matthew Diamond, Joseph Behar, Danielle Faraldo, Craig McManus, William Ludel, Phideaux Xavier, Scott McKinsey, Owen Renfroe, Penny Pengra, Christine Magarian, Ron Cates, Peter Fillmore, Ronald C. Cates, Dave MacLeod
- Head Writer: Robert Guza, Jr.
- **Associate Head Writer/Script Editor:** Elizabeth Korte
- **Story Consultant:** Brian Frons
- **Breakdown Writers:** Jim Reitzel, Michael Conforti, Heidi Ploen, Sasha Cartullo, Nathan Fissel, David Goldschmid, Meg Bennett
- **Script Writers:** Susan Wald (playwright), Michele Val Jean, Mary Sue Price, Karen Harris, Elizabeth Korte
- **Casting Directors**: Mark Teschner, Gwen Hillier
- Former Notable Crew Members: John William Corrington, Lewis Arlt [3], Lynda Myles [4], Alan Pultz, Judith Pinsker [5], Joseph Behar [6], Stephanie Braxton [7], Norma Monty, Frank South [8], Ralph Ellis [9], Shelley Curtis [10], Hope Harmel Smith

Setting

Many sites in Port Charles include:

- General Hospital is a major employer in the city, and one of the largest medical facilities on the East Coast. With contributions from Sonny Corinthos and Carly Jacks, extra wings dedicated to AIDS research and pediatric head neurology have been constructed. In 2009, a vicious fire destroyed a majority of the hospital, which was promptly rebuilt. The hospital re-opened in April.
- The Metro Court is the most prominent hotel in Port Charles, owned by entrepreneurs Jasper Jacks and Carly Corinthos. When the Port Charles Hotel was destroyed by a fire in 2004, the Metro Court was built on its site. The hotel boasts a skyline restaurant, a world-class spa, and multiple penthouse suites.
- Kelly's Diner is a vintage restaurant in the heart of Port Charles. Operated by Mike Corbin, the diner has been serving its devoted patrons since 1978. The lofts above Kelly's have been home to hundreds of tenants over the years, although the rooms are currently vacant.
- The Haunted Star is a yacht owned and operated by Luke Spencer, who received the vessel as a wedding present in 1983. In 2003, the ship was turned into a casino by Luke and investors Skye Chandler and Tracy Quartermaine.
- Jake's is a bar located in downtown Port Charles, just a block away from General Hospital. Since the early '90s, the bar has been a hotspot for the local nightlife. Coleman Ratcliffe has owned the bar since 2002.

Prominent families include the Quartermaines, the Cassadines, the Spencers, and the Corinthoses.

Awards

Daytime Emmy Award wins

Drama series and performer categories

- Drama Series: Gloria Monty 1981, 1984; Wendy Riche 1995, 1996, 1997, 1999, 2000; Jill Farren Phelps 2005, 2006, 2008
- Lead Actor: Anthony Geary (Luke Spencer) 1982, 1999, 2000, 2004, 2006, 2008; Maurice Benard (Sonny Corinthos) 2003
- Lead Actress: Finola Hughes (Anna Devane) 1991
- Supporting Actor: Peter Hansen (Lee Baldwin) 1979; David Lewis (Edward Quartermaine) 1982; Gerald Anthony (Marco Dane) 1993; Steve Burton (Jason Morgan) 1998; Stuart Damon (Alan Quartermaine) 1999; Rick Hearst (Ric Lansing) 2004, 2007
- Supporting Actress: Jane Elliot (Tracy Quartermaine) 1981; Rena Sofer (Lois Cerullo) 1995; Sarah Brown (Carly Benson) 2000; Vanessa Marcil (Brenda Barrett), 2003; Natalia Livingston (Emily Quartermaine), 2005; Genie Francis (Laura Spencer), 2007;

- Younger Actor: Jonathan Jackson (Lucky Spencer) 1995, 1998, 1999; Jacob Young (Lucky Spencer) 2002; Chad Brannon (Zander Smith) 2004
- Younger Actress: Kimberly McCullough (Robin Scorpio) 1989, 1996; Sarah Brown (Carly Benson) 1997, 1998; Julie Marie Berman (Lulu Spencer), 2009, 2010
- Lifetime Achievement: Rachel Ames (Audrey March Hardy) 2004; Anna Lee (Lila Quartermaine) 2004 (posthumous)

Other categories

- 2010 "Outstanding Drama Series Directing Team"
- 2009 "Outstanding Drama Series Writing Team"
- 2008 "Outstanding Achievement in Casting for a Drama Series"
- 2007 "Outstanding Achievement in Casting for a Drama Series"
- 2006 "Outstanding Drama Series Directing Team"
- 2006 "Outstanding Achievement in Casting for a Drama Series"
- 2006 "Outstanding Achievement in Hairstyling for a Drama Series"
- 2005 "Outstanding Drama Series Directing Team"
- 2004 "Outstanding Drama Series Directing Team"
- 2004 "Outstanding Achievement in Makeup for a Drama Series"
- 2003 "Outstanding Drama Series Writing Team"
- 2004 "Lifetime Achievement 2003 "Outstanding Achievement in Multiple Camera Editing for a Drama Series"
- 2002 "Outstanding Original Song"
- 2000 "Outstanding Drama Series Directing Team"
- 1999 "Outstanding Drama Series Writing Team"
- 1999 "Outstanding Achievement in Makeup for a Drama Series"
- 1999 "Outstanding Achievement in Costume Design for a Drama Series"
- 1999 "Outstanding Original Song" (TIED with *As the World Turns*)
- 1998 "Outstanding Achievement in Costume Design for a Drama Series"
- 1996 "Outstanding Achievement in Costume Design for a Drama Series"
- 1995 "Outstanding Drama Series Writing Team"
- 1995 "Outstanding Achievement in Costume Design for a Drama Series"
- 1982 "Outstanding Drama Series Directing Team"
- 1981 "Outstanding Drama Series Directing Team"

Directors Guild of America

- 1996, 1998, 2002, and 2004 "Outstanding Directorial Achievement in Daytime Serials.-.-.-.

Writers Guild of America

- 1995, 1996, and 1998 "Daytime Serials"

Broadcast history

When ABC premiered *General Hospital* on April 1, 1963, the network placed it in the 1 p.m./12 Noon Central timeslot against local newscasts on NBC and CBS affiliates. But on December 30 of that year, *General Hospital* assumed a place on the daytime schedule that, except for almost seventeen months between July 1976 and January 1978 when it ran as one half of a 90-minute bloc with *One Life to Live* between 2:30/1:30 and 4/3, it has maintained to this day, 3/2 Central.

During the 1960s, *General Hospital* earned decent ratings against the likes of *To Tell the Truth* and *The Secret Storm* on CBS, but there was a decline as the 1970s came, especially when NBC's *Another World* became highly popular; for two years, it also faced CBS' *The Price Is Right*, already a major hit. After continued mediocrity in the Nielsen ratings, ABC was prepared to cancel *General Hospital*, but decided to give it a second chance in 1978 when it expanded the show to a full hour, from an experimental 45 minutes. However, the expansion came with an ultimatum to the producers that they had six months to improve the show's ratings. Head writers Douglas Marland & Gloria Monty were hired as executive producers, and on their first day, they spent an extra $100,000 re-taping four episodes. A miracle occurred thanks to Monty and the show became the most watched daytime drama by 1979, marking a rare instance of a daytime serial's comeback from near-extinction. During the wedding of Luke and Laura Spencer on November 16, 1981, about 30 million people tuned in to watch them exchange vows and be cursed by Elizabeth Taylor's Helena Cassadine (later played by Constance Towers).

From 1979 to 1988, *General Hospital* remained number one in the ratings, competing against two low-rated soaps on NBC -- *Texas* and *Santa Barbara* -- and the long-running *Guiding Light* (*GL*) over on CBS (although, it should be noted, that for a brief period in the middle of 1984, *Guiding Light* experienced a renaissance and became the #1 soap, dethroning *General Hospital* from the top ratings spot, thanks to well-regarded storylines written by then-*GL* head writer Pam Long). For the most part, however, *General Hospital* continued to triumph, even after the departure of popular actors Anthony Geary and Genie Francis in the mid-1980s. Although *The Young and the Restless* took *General Hospital's* place as the highest-rated serial in 1989, *General Hospital* continued to maintain excellent ratings.

Ever since the 1991-1992 season of *General Hospital*, the show has had a steady decline in ratings. On and off they would be in between third and fifth place in the Nielsen Ratings, placing CBS's *The Young*

And The Restless and *The Bold and the Beautiful* in first and second place, respectively. *General Hospital* still remains in between third and fifth place in the ratings to this day. During the 1990s *General Hospital* was put up against fellow soap opera, *All My Children*, CBS's *As the World Turns* and NBC's *Days of our Lives*.

Ratings History

Highest-rated week in daytime history (November 16–20, 1981)

(Household ratings, Nielsen Media Research)

Years as #1 series

Year(s)	Household Rating
1979-1980	9.9
1980–1981	11.4
1981–1982	11.2
1982–1983	9.8
1983–1984	10.0
1984–1985	9.1
1985–1986	9.2
1986–1987	8.3
1987–1988	8.1 (Tied with *The Young and the Restless*)

Serial	Household rating	(Time slot) Network	Millions of households
1. *General Hospital*	16.0	(3-4pm) ABC	17.5
2. *All My Children*	10.2	(1-2pm) ABC	11.7
3. *One Life To Live*	10.2	(2-3pm) ABC	11.6
4. *Guiding Light*	7.9	(3-4pm) CBS	8.2

1962-1963 season

- 1. *As the World Turns* 13.7
- 9. *General Hospital* 3.9 (Debut)

1963-1964 season

- 1. *As the World Turns* 15.4
- 7. *General Hospital* 5.4

1964-1965 season

- 1. *As the World Turns* 14.5
- 7. *General Hospital* 8.0

1965-1966 season

- 1. *As the World Turns* 13.9
- 7. *General Hospital* 7.3

1966-1967 season

- 1. *As the World Turns* 12.7
- 9. *General Hospital* 7.0

1967-1968 season

- 1. *As the World Turns* 13.6
- 9. *General Hospital* 8.8

1968-1969 season

- 1. *As the World Turns* 13.8
- 10. *General Hospital* 8.8

1969-1970 season

- 1. *As the World Turns* 13.6
- 10. *General Hospital* 8.5

1970-1971 season

- 1. *As the World Turns* 12.4
- 4. *General Hospital* 9.5 (Tied with *Another World* and *Days of our Lives*)

1971-1972 season

- 1. *As the World Turns* 11.1
- 2. *General Hospital* 10.4

1972-1973 season

- 1. *As the World Turns* 10.6
- 2. *General Hospital* 9.7 (Tied with *Another World*)

1973-1974 season

- 1. *As the World Turns* 10.6 (Tied with *Days of our Lives* and *Another World*)
- 5. *General Hospital* 9.2

1974-1975 season

- 1. *As the World Turns* 10.8
- 7. *General Hospital* 8.5 (Tied with *Guiding Light*)

1975-1976 season

- 1. *As the World Turns* 9.4
- 10. *General Hospital* 7.1

1976-1977 season

- 1. *As the World Turns* 9.9
- 10. *General Hospital* 7.0

1977-1978 season

- 1. *As the World Turns* 8.6 (Tied with *Another World*)
- 10. *General Hospital* 7.1

1978-1979 season

- 1. *All My Children* 9.0
- 2. *General Hospital* 8.7

1988-1989 season

- 1. *The Young and the Restless* 8.1
- 2. *General Hospital* 7.5

1989-1990 season

1989-1990 season

- 1. *The Young and the Restless* 8.0
- 2. *General Hospital* 7.4

1990-1991 season

- 1. *The Young and the Restless* 8.1
- 2. *General Hospital* 6.7

1991-1992 ratings

- 1. *The Young and the Restless* 8.2
- 3. *General Hospital* 5.8 (Tied with *As the World Turns*)

1992-1993 ratings

- 1. *The Young and the Restless* 8.4
- 3. *General Hospital* 5.8

1993-1994 ratings

- 1. *The Young and the Restless* 8.6
- 3. *General Hospital* 4.7

1994-1995 ratings

- 1. *The Young and the Restless* 7.5
- 3. *General Hospital* 5.6

1995-1996 ratings

- 1. *The Young and the Restless* 7.7
- 5. *General Hospital* 4.7

1996-1997 season

- 1. *The Young and the Restless* 7.1
- 4. *General Hospital* 4.8

1997-1998 season

- 1. *The Young and the Restless* 7.0
- 4. *General Hospital* 4.7

1998-1999 season

- 1. *The Young and the Restless* 6.9
- 4. *General Hospital* 4.6

1999-2000 season

- 1. *The Young and the Restless* 6.8
- 4. *General Hospital* 4.0

2000-2001 season

- 1. *The Young and the Restless* 5.8
- 4. *General Hospital* 3.7

2001-2002 season

- 1. *The Young and the Restless* 5.0
- 4. *General Hospital* 3.4

2002-2003 season

- 1. *The Young and the Restless* 4.7
- 3. *General Hospital* 3.5

2003-2004 season

- 1. *The Young and the Restless* 4.4
- 3. *General Hospital* 3.2

2004-2005 season

- 1. *The Young and the Restless* 4.2
- 3. *General Hospital* 3.0

2005-2006 season

- 1. *The Young and the Restless* 4.2
- 3. *General Hospital* 2.7

2006-2007 season

- 1. *The Young and the Restless* 4.2
- 3. *General Hospital* 2.6

2007-2008 season

- 1. *The Young and the Restless* 4.0
- 4. *General Hospital* 2.3

2008-2009 season

- 1. *The Young and the Restless* 3.7
- 3. *General Hospital* 2.1

2009-2010 season As of ratings for July 4, 2010

- 1. *The Young and the Restless* 3.8 (As of July 4, 2010)
- 4. *General Hospital* 2.1 (As of July 4, 2010)

With the show still number one in the Nielsens, WDTN in Dayton, Ohio canceled GH in May 1983 in favor of Woody Woodpecker and SuperFriends cartoons. Later, the station would air such shows as *Hour Magazine*, *Geraldo* and *Maury* in GH's time slot until September 2000, when the station's new owners, Sunrise Broadcasting, canceled Maury, due to what it called "community standards", and brought GH back.

Cultural influence

The popularity of *General Hospital* has gained it many parodies and references in other mainstream programs. For example, in the early 1990s, some episodes of *General Hospital* were featured as "shorts" during the fourth season of the parody show *Mystery Science Theater 3000*. The series was also parodied/homaged in the song *General Hospi-Tale* by The Afternoon Delights, and in the film *Tootsie*, which took place among the cast and crew of a fictional soap opera program. In the Fox medical drama *House*, Dr. House enjoys *Prescription: Passion*, which is a poorly acted, over-the-top parody of *General Hospital* that he watches constantly, even when he should be working. In the season three episode, "Half-Wit", House hides his blood test results under the name, "Luke N. Laura", referring to *General Hospital*'s legendary couple. MAD TV did a sketch on the series with actors Jacklyn Zeman, Rebecca Herbst, and Jacob Young (the second Lucky). The movie *Young Doctors in Love* featured a large part of General Hospital's cast from 1982. In a 2010 episode of *The Colbert Report*, comedian Stephen Colbert poked fun at the show, responding to a clip of Maurice Benard's Sonny shooting Dominic Zamprogna's Dante, saying "Sonny shot Dante! No!"

Famous fans

General Hospital has many famous fans, including Wayne Gretzky and his wife, Janet Jones, along with *The Sopranos* actor Vincent Pastore, who would join the show in late 2008 for a short guest stint. World renowned skier Kristi Leskinen is a devout fan of the show, along with actor Jason Gray-Stanford and singer Billy Currington. Laura Wright, *General Hospital*'s Carly, was a huge fan of the show in the 1980s before joining the cast in 2005. Motocross driver Mike Metzger is also a fan of the program, and rarely missing an episode. Elizabeth Taylor, a huge fan of the show, asked for a role on the soap opera and joined the cast temporarily as Helena Cassadine to be a part of Luke and Laura's 1981 wedding. Surprisingly, Princess Diana was a devout fan of the show, and went as far as to send two bottles of Bollinger champagne to Anthony Geary and Genie Francis in time for Luke and Laura's 1981 wedding. Geary turned his into a lamp. Diana's wedding to Prince Charles earlier that year outrated Luke and Laura's in number of viewers. *General Hospital* helped launch the singing career of Rick Springfield, who had watched the show for many years before joining the series in 1981. While never having sang on the show, his name recognition brought him substantial notoriety in the music community. On the July 5, 2010, episode of *The Colbert Report*, comedian Stephen Colbert told his audience that being on sick leave allowed him to catch up on *General Hospital*. The fictional diagnostician Gregory House on the popular TV series *House, M.D.* is portrayed as an avid fan of *General Hospital*.

Spin-offs and specials

The success of the long-running soap opera has had one sister soap, one spin-off in the United States, and two primetime spin-offs in the U.S. and the United Kingdom.

The Young Marrieds (1964–1966) was ABC's first attempt at a sister soap for *General Hospital*. It ran for only two years, racking up a total of only 380 episodes. Despite its moderate popularity, it was put up against CBS's top-rated *The Edge of Night*, which it could not compete against. The series finale aired on March 25, 1966, with the show's main protagonist contemplating suicide. It ended in a cliffhanger, leaving the audience wondering if the man had killed himself or not. *The Young Marrieds* was set in the fictional suburb of Queen's Point, which was considered by the writers to be a suburb of Port Charles. Many fans consider Robin Scorpio and Elizabeth Webber's homes to be in this area of the town.

The U.K. series *General Hospital* (1972–1979) did not feature any characters from the American show, but was modeled after its format. It started as a half-hour program broadcast in the afternoons, which was unusual for UK serials that normally aired in prime time. In 1975 it was expanded to an hour-long format and moved to Friday evenings.

Port Charles (1997–2003) was a daytime drama that initially featured interns in a competitive medical school program, and was known for having more action actually in the hospital than *General Hospital* itself. It also included the characters of Scott Baldwin. Serena Baldwin, Lucy Coe, Kevin Collins, and Karen Wexler, all of whom originally appeared as characters on *General Hospital*. As the show evolved, it tended more towards gothic intrigue, including supernatural elements such as vampires and life after death. It also switched formats from an open-ended daytime serial to 13-week story arcs known as "books", similar to Spanish language telenovelas.

General Hospital: Night Shift (2007–2008) is the second American prime time spin-off of a daytime drama (the first being *Our Private World*, a spin-off of *As the World Turns*). Its first season aired from July 12, 2007 to October 4, 2007 on SOAPnet, a cable channel owned by ABC. The series follows the nighttime adventures of familiar and new characters around the hospital. As of March 2008, the first season of the series was "SOAPnet's most-watched series ever", with ABC Daytime and SOAPnet President Brian Frons noting that *Night Shift* drew more than 1 million new viewers to the channel during its first season.

General Hospital: Twist of Fate (1996) was a primetime special that aired on Saturday, December 14, 1996. The episode picked up where that Friday's show had left off. The special centered around Laura's supposed death at the hands of Stefan Cassadine.

On April 2, 1998, *General Hospital* aired a primetime special in celebration of the program's 35th anniversary. Hosted by Anthony Geary, the show focused and recapped on many popular storylines including Monica's breast cancer, BJ's death, and Stone's battle with HIV. To date, this is the only anniversary special that was broadcast in primetime and that didn't include any of the current storyline.

Bibliography

- Gary Warner, *General Hospital: The Complete Scrapbook*, Stoddart (November 1995), ISBN 1881649407
- Gerard J. Waggett, *The Official General Hospital Trivia Book*, ABC (October 1997), ISBN 0786882751

External links

- Watch "General Hospital" Episodes Online [1]
- *General Hospital* [11] at the Internet Movie Database
- *General Hospital* [12] at TV.com

Article Sources and Contributors

The Young and the Restless *Source*: http://en.wikipedia.org/?oldid=389397723 *Contributors*: Ckatz

List of The Young and the Restless characters *Source*: http://en.wikipedia.org/?oldid=390614665 *Contributors*: 1 anonymous edits

List of The Young and the Restless cast members *Source*: http://en.wikipedia.org/?oldid=390589624 *Contributors*: 1 anonymous edits

Jeanne Cooper *Source*: http://en.wikipedia.org/?oldid=384223862 *Contributors*: 1 anonymous edits

Doug Davidson *Source*: http://en.wikipedia.org/?oldid=386039574 *Contributors*: 1 anonymous edits

Melody Thomas Scott *Source*: http://en.wikipedia.org/?oldid=390534565 *Contributors*: 1 anonymous edits

Eric Braeden *Source*: http://en.wikipedia.org/?oldid=386896132 *Contributors*: MrKing84

Eileen Davidson *Source*: http://en.wikipedia.org/?oldid=386188057 *Contributors*:

Kate Linder *Source*: http://en.wikipedia.org/?oldid=386994061 *Contributors*:

Tracey E. Bregman *Source*: http://en.wikipedia.org/?oldid=390638400 *Contributors*: 1 anonymous edits

Jess Walton *Source*: http://en.wikipedia.org/?oldid=386697007 *Contributors*:

Peter Bergman *Source*: http://en.wikipedia.org/?oldid=384341680 *Contributors*: Hargrimm

Kristoff St. John *Source*: http://en.wikipedia.org/?oldid=383986226 *Contributors*: 1 anonymous edits

All My Children *Source*: http://en.wikipedia.org/?oldid=390353549 *Contributors*: Saint Crimson

One Life to Live *Source*: http://en.wikipedia.org/?oldid=390645710 *Contributors*: TAnthony

General Hospital *Source*: http://en.wikipedia.org/?oldid=390646333 *Contributors*: TAnthony

Image Sources, Licenses and Contributors

File:Flag of Australia.svg *Source*: http://bibliocm.bibliolabs.com/mwAnon/index.php?title=File:Flag_of_Australia.svg *License*: Public Domain *Contributors*: Ian Fieggen

File:Flag of Belgium (civil).svg *Source*: http://bibliocm.bibliolabs.com/mwAnon/index.php?title=File:Flag_of_Belgium_(civil).svg *License*: Public Domain *Contributors*: Bean49, David Descamps, Dbenbenn, Denelson83, Fry1989, Gabriel trzy, Howcome, Ms2ger, Nightstallion, Oreo Priest, Rocket000, Sir Iain, ThomasPusch, Warddr, Zscout370, 4 anonymous edits

File:Flag of Brazil.svg *Source*: http://bibliocm.bibliolabs.com/mwAnon/index.php?title=File:Flag_of_Brazil.svg *License*: Public Domain *Contributors*: Brazilian Government

File:Flag of Canada.svg *Source*: http://bibliocm.bibliolabs.com/mwAnon/index.php?title=File:Flag_of_Canada.svg *License*: Public Domain *Contributors*: User:E Pluribus Anthony, User:Mzajac

File:Flag of Finland.svg *Source*: http://bibliocm.bibliolabs.com/mwAnon/index.php?title=File:Flag_of_Finland.svg *License*: Public Domain *Contributors*: User:SKopp

File:Flag of France.svg *Source*: http://bibliocm.bibliolabs.com/mwAnon/index.php?title=File:Flag_of_France.svg *License*: Public Domain *Contributors*: User:SKopp, User:SKopp, User:SKopp, User:SKopp, User:SKopp, User:SKopp

File:Flag of Germany.svg *Source*: http://bibliocm.bibliolabs.com/mwAnon/index.php?title=File:Flag_of_Germany.svg *License*: Public Domain *Contributors*: User:Madden, User:Pumbaa80, User:SKopp

File:Flag of Greece.svg *Source*: http://bibliocm.bibliolabs.com/mwAnon/index.php?title=File:Flag_of_Greece.svg *License*: Public Domain *Contributors*: (of code) (talk)

File:Flag of India.svg *Source*: http://bibliocm.bibliolabs.com/mwAnon/index.php?title=File:Flag_of_India.svg *License*: Public Domain *Contributors*: User:SKopp

File:Flag of Italy.svg *Source*: http://bibliocm.bibliolabs.com/mwAnon/index.php?title=File:Flag_of_Italy.svg *License*: Public Domain *Contributors*: see below

File:Flag of Jamaica.svg *Source*: http://bibliocm.bibliolabs.com/mwAnon/index.php?title=File:Flag_of_Jamaica.svg *License*: Public Domain *Contributors*: User:Madden

File:Flag of Macedonia.svg *Source*: http://bibliocm.bibliolabs.com/mwAnon/index.php?title=File:Flag_of_Macedonia.svg *License*: Public Domain *Contributors*: User:Gabbe, User:SKopp

File:Flag of New Zealand.svg *Source*: http://bibliocm.bibliolabs.com/mwAnon/index.php?title=File:Flag_of_New_Zealand.svg *License*: Public Domain *Contributors*: Adambro, Arria Belli, Avenue, Bawolff, Bjankuloski06en, ButterStick, Denelson83, Donk, Duduziq, EugeneZelenko, Fred J, Fry1989, Hugh Jass, Ibagli, Jusjih, Klemen Kocjancic, Mamndassan, Mattes, Nightstallion, O, Peeperman, Poromiami, Reisio, Rfc1394, Shizhao, Tabasco, Transparent Blue, Väsk, Xufanc, Zscout370, 35 anonymous edits

File:Flag of Romania.svg *Source*: http://bibliocm.bibliolabs.com/mwAnon/index.php?title=File:Flag_of_Romania.svg *License*: Public Domain *Contributors*: User:AdiJapan

File:Flag of Norway.svg *Source*: http://bibliocm.bibliolabs.com/mwAnon/index.php?title=File:Flag_of_Norway.svg *License*: Public Domain *Contributors*: User:Dbenbenn

File:Flag of Poland.svg *Source*: http://bibliocm.bibliolabs.com/mwAnon/index.php?title=File:Flag_of_Poland.svg *License*: Public Domain *Contributors*: User:Mareklug, User:Wanted

File:Flag of the Philippines.svg *Source*: http://bibliocm.bibliolabs.com/mwAnon/index.php?title=File:Flag_of_the_Philippines.svg *License*: Public Domain *Contributors*: Aira Cutamora

File:Flag of Serbia.svg *Source*: http://bibliocm.bibliolabs.com/mwAnon/index.php?title=File:Flag_of_Serbia.svg *License*: Public Domain *Contributors*: ABF, Avala, B1mbo, Denelson83, EDUCA33E, Fry1989, Herbythyme, Homo lupus, Imbris, Maks Stirlitz, Mormegil, Nightstallion, Nikola Smolenski, Nuno Gabriel Cabral, Odder, R-41, Rainman, Rokerismoravee, Sasa Stefanovic, Siebrand, TFCforever, ThomasPusch, Túrelio, Zscout370, 7 anonymous edits

File:Flag of Slovenia.svg *Source*: http://bibliocm.bibliolabs.com/mwAnon/index.php?title=File:Flag_of_Slovenia.svg *License*: Public Domain *Contributors*: User:SKopp, User:Vzb83, User:Zscout370

File:Flag of South Africa.svg *Source*: http://bibliocm.bibliolabs.com/mwAnon/index.php?title=File:Flag_of_South_Africa.svg *License*: unknown *Contributors*: Adriaan, Anime Addict AA, AnonMoos, BRUTE, Daemonic Kangaroo, Dnik, Duduziq, Dzordzm, Fry1989, Homo lupus, Jappalang, Juliancolton, Kam Solusar, Klemen Kocjancic, Klymene, Lexxyy, Mahahahaneapneap, Manuelt15, Moviedefender, NeverDoING, Ninane, Poznaniak, SKopp, ThePCKid, ThomasPusch, Tvdm, Ultratomio, Vzb83, Zscout370, 33 anonymous edits

File:Flag of Sweden.svg *Source*: http://bibliocm.bibliolabs.com/mwAnon/index.php?title=File:Flag_of_Sweden.svg *License*: Public Domain *Contributors*: User:Jon Harald Søby

File:Flag of Switzerland.svg *Source*: http://bibliocm.bibliolabs.com/mwAnon/index.php?title=File:Flag_of_Switzerland.svg *License*: Public Domain *Contributors*: User:-xfi-, User:Marc Mongenet, User:Zscout370

File:Flag of Turkey.svg *Source*: http://bibliocm.bibliolabs.com/mwAnon/index.php?title=File:Flag_of_Turkey.svg *License*: Public Domain *Contributors*: User:Dbenbenn

File:Flag of the Czech Republic.svg *Source*: http://bibliocm.bibliolabs.com/mwAnon/index.php?title=File:Flag_of_the_Czech_Republic.svg *License*: Public Domain *Contributors*: special commission (of code): SVG version by cs:-xfi-. Colors according to Appendix No. 3 of czech legal Act 3/1993. cs:Zirland.

File:Eric Braeden (Los Angeles, July 2007).jpg *Source*: http://bibliocm.bibliolabs.com/mwAnon/index.php?title=File:Eric_Braeden_(Los_Angeles,_July_2007).jpg *License*: Creative Commons Attribution 2.0 *Contributors*: Stefan Kloo from Los Angeles

File:Kate Linder LF.JPG *Source*: http://bibliocm.bibliolabs.com/mwAnon/index.php?title=File:Kate_Linder_LF.JPG *License*: unknown *Contributors*: lukeford.net